STILL LIFE IN HARLEM

I came up from the subway and into the bright light of day. I felt a little of what Langston Hughes must have felt when he first arrived in Harlem in 1922. It was a bright September afternoon that greeted me, a bright September afternoon that greeted him. And as he was happy and thrilled to be here, so was I, though probably not as much, for in 1922 Harlem was still young and new and its magic had yet to be tarnished. Langston Hughes was so delirious on coming here, he later wrote, that he was never able to capture on paper the excitement even of riding the subway uptown.

"I went up the steps," he said, "and out into the bright September sunlight. Harlem! I stood there, dropped my bags, took a deep breath and felt happy again."

I was happy to be here too.

Still Life in Harlem

EDDY L. HARRIS

Henry Holt and Company   New York

Henry Holt and Company, Inc.
Publishers since 1866
115 West 18th Street
New York, New York 10011

Henry Holt® is a registered
trademark of Henry Holt and Company, Inc.

Library of Congress Cataloging-in-Publication Data
Harris, Eddy L.
Still life in Harlem / Eddy L. Harris.—1st ed.
p.   cm.
1. Harlem (New York, N.Y.)—Description and travel.   2. Harlem
(New York, N.Y.)—Social conditions.   3. Afro-Americans—New York
(State)—New York—Social conditions.   4. New York (N.Y.)—
Description and travel.   5. New York (N.Y.)—Social conditions.
I. Title.
F128.68.H3H37   1996   96-23771
974.7′100496073—dc20   CIP

ISBN 0-8050-4851-0

Henry Holt books are available for special promotions and
premiums. For details contact: Director, Special Markets.

First Edition—1996

Designed by Kate Nichols

Printed in the United States of America
All first editions are printed on acid-free paper. ∞

1   3   5   7   9   10   8   6   4   2

To Inge Rew Hanson,
whose love and support sustain me.

Thanks as well to Clare Alexander,
who saw what I could not see,
and to Amanda Whitley.

STILL LIFE IN HARLEM

I know what the caged bird feels, alas!
When the sun is bright on the upland slopes;
When the wind stirs soft through the springing grass,
And the river flows like a stream of glass;
When the first bird sings and the first bud opes,
And the faint perfume from its chalice steals—
I know what the caged bird feels!

I know why the caged bird beats his wing
Till its blood is red on the cruel bars;
For he must fly back to his perch and cling
When he fain would be on the bough a-swing;
And a pain still throbs in the old, old scars
And they pulse again with a keener sting—
I know why he beats his wing!

I know why the caged bird sings, ah me,
When his wing is bruised and his bosom sore,—
When he beats his bars and he would be free;
It is not a carol of joy or glee,
But a prayer that he sends from his heart's deep core,
But a plea, that upward to Heaven he flings—
I know why the caged bird sings!

—Paul Laurence Dunbar, "Sympathy"

*T*oward the end of my second year living in Harlem, I was awakened in the middle of the night by a woman's voice screaming inside my head. The panic in her shouting came echoing faintly as if from out of a dream. I tried to shake myself loose from this dream, but the screaming would not stop. When I realized it was not a dream, I sat up in bed, listened for a minute, then tried once more to go back to sleep.

Many times I had heard wild rantings such as these coming through an open window. Nearly every weekend in fact, from somewhere in my apartment building or in the building across the way, a drunken couple would spend hours deep in the night hurling abuse at each other. She would end each session by throwing her lover out. He, having had enough, would always leave. Somehow, though, he would be there again the following night and the next weekend too, drunk the two of them and at it again.

When I awoke a second time, a brief minute or two later, I realized there was nothing I recognized in the shrieking. I wasn't so sure now that it came from the couple across the courtyard.

At first I tried to ignore it. I couldn't. Groggy but fully awake, I tried again to listen. I had no idea where the fighting was coming from.

There is a strange way sound bounces around outside my windows and enters the apartment. The windows in the front room open onto the street. Then comes the room where I sleep, a bedroom in the center of this long but narrow four-room apartment. The windows in the bedroom open onto a courtyardlike space between this building and the building next door. When you first hear sounds coming from the outside, very often you cannot tell if they enter the apartment from the courtyard or if they come from the street. I had to get up to find out.

I went to the bedroom window and heard nothing. I went to the front room and did the same, stuck my head out the window, and again heard no voices.

I could see nothing through the glare of the street lamp that stood just outside my front-room window. I shielded my eyes from the light but still saw nothing, no sign of struggle, nothing but a picture-perfect night in the city.

The night was cool. Autumn was coming on. There was no moon, no stars, no clouds. All was still and quiet along the street. The only sound came from the papers and the leaves that rustled in the slight breeze that now gathered and drifted gently.

A few seconds later, there it was: the screaming again. The moment of calm was splintered. I shielded my eyes once more. Now accustomed at once to the darkness and to

4

the harsh glow from the street lamp, I could see all I needed to see. There in the shadows across the street was the beginning of the end of my life in Harlem.

The beginning of the end too, I told myself, of my being black. After this, I had had enough. I wanted no more of it.

It was quite a moment, that moment of calm, that moment of clarity when everything seemed to crystallize, a moment of utter serenity turning into utmost rage, that moment when the water boils.

I remember thinking only seconds before what a beautiful place Harlem must have been at one time and wondering where the beauty went. To be fair and honest, there is beauty here. There simply isn't enough of it to counterbalance what has become so lifeless, so tired, and so ugly. There is still life in Harlem, certainly, but there is a barrenness to it.

Up the street from where I live stand a handful of magnificent stone buildings.

Down the street from where I live, a man the other day was killing rats.

And across the street from where I live, a man this night was bashing a woman against a stone wall. He was exhibiting his power, pounding out of her the respect the world had pounded out of him, demanding with each well-placed blow the same submission from her that had been demanded of him; to demonstrate to this woman and to himself that here in these shadows, if nowhere else, he was in control and had some control over his life and somebody else's.

The man was black. The woman—she was black too.

And what in the world was I supposed to do? I felt as

helpless as I had been those many many years before, when I had taken my first backward steps out of the darkness that was becoming the world of blackness.

How long—how long it has been and how far I have gone in trying at the same time to come closer and to put distance between my world and that world, both to remember and to put the memory out of my mind. Even now the memory is painful, and it makes me wince.

When I was nine years old I watched one black man stab another black man. Nothing I had seen or ever heard up until then could possibly have prepared me for the senselessness of this act, for the man doing the stabbing did what he did just for the fun of it. His victim had already been stabbed in a fight with someone else. Then along came this Johnny Cannon, a neighborhood toughie who had been in and out of reformatory and prison several times already and who later would steal my watch at a party.

Johnny Cannon had watched the fight. He might even have egged it on, but he had not been part of it. Nevertheless, he got into it now.

When the fight was over, the loser was dragged out of Kirksey's Confectionary, where the argument had taken place. He was laid on the front steps. He had already been stabbed once in the belly, and as this man lay there bleeding, Johnny Cannon knelt down beside him, pulled out a knife, and plunged it into the other man's chest. Then Johnny pushed and twisted the knife until the blade snapped off and remained buried in the dying man's body. Then Johnny laughed.

I should have cried, I guess, but I did not. I should have

run, gone home, buried my face in my mother's lap, and sobbed as she stroked my head to soothe me. She would have offered me oatmeal cookies with which to erase the acid taste rising in my throat, and perhaps I would have forgotten all about the horror and stupidity I had just seen. But I did not go home. I got no cookies. And I never ever forgot.

I stood there transfixed, so stunned that I could neither move nor turn my eyes away. I watched every move anyone made and committed to memory these components of a world I decided even then, at this early age, that I wanted no part of.

I heard the sirens of police cars approaching from the south. A small crowd had gathered, blocking my view. I had to squeeze to the side in order to watch what was going on. From there I could see the eager faces of those gathered as the bleeding man's limp body was loaded into the backseat of a car. Someone shouted, "Put his head in a plastic bag." Just before they sped away, cops on their tails, tires smoking, squealing, burning rubber, the two men who had done the stabbing, Johnny Cannon and the other fellow whom I had never seen before and have not seen since, looked in my direction and caught my eye.

As I think back now, I search my memory for an appeal in their eyes, a plea for me who had seen it all to keep silent. There was no plea. There was no pain no joy no look of satisfaction. There was nothing at all, an emptiness devoid even of desperation.

It was a look of resignation and of surrender. *This is how it is,* they seemed to be saying. This is how it is.

From my Harlem apartment that late night and early morning I was too far away to see much of anything. Shadows were shoving shadows, that's all, and being shoved in return. But if I could have seen the face of the man that late night, I am sure that in his eyes would have been the same expression, some rage perhaps, for he was certainly angered, but with the rage the same look of surrender and resignation even as he tried to force this woman to submit to his will.

"Leave me alone," she cried. "Leave me alone!"

Over and over she pleaded, the same words, the same shriek, the same shrill voice, until the man hit her once too hard and she dropped from her arms whatever it was that he wanted her to give him.

Now he was outraged even further, and he demanded that she pick it up. When she would not, he smacked her head and shoved her hard against the wall. I heard her feeble moan as the wind was knocked out of her.

What was I supposed to do? Surely this was not the time nor the place for heroics. I had seen by then too many guns in too many hot hands in Harlem. I had been shot at, though only once, and I had been lucky. That one time was more than enough. I did not want there to be a second time.

I dialed the emergency number for the police. Then I waited for them to come. There was nothing more I could reasonably do. I was trapped—as trapped as the woman who could not escape, as trapped by what he was doing as the man who was beating her, as trapped by what had been done to him.

Though I could not see it, I could feel this look of surrender in his eyes. I had seen it enough to know that it was there.

Harlem.

Down the street from where I live, I watched a man the other day killing rats. In front of his apartment building there are no trash cans for the people who live there. Instead they put their garbage in the three black plastic bags that hang from the chain link fence. The fence blocks off the vacant lot next door.

This vacant lot, like all the vacant lots in the neighborhood, is a receptacle for debris. People as they pass toss empty bottles and cans over the fence. Loose pieces of paper, candy wrappers, potato chip bags, old newspapers: all get thrown into the lot along with half-eaten sandwiches, apple cores and banana peels, tree branches and piles of wood and large chunks of concrete from some building being torn down somewhere. Around the trash and the rubble, weeds grow ragged where there might once have been grass, or where there could be even now if anyone cared enough about anything so simple as beauty. No one does—or no one seems to—and the debris piles up almost unnoticed, giving the rats that live in the buildings on either side of this vacant lot a place to search for food and plenty of daytime cover. The boldest ones, though, don't need the cover. They venture right out into the open.

Several of these rats had climbed the lower links of the fence and had gnawed into the plastic bags hanging there. Once inside, the rats were trapped. As they feasted on the garbage inside, a man took down one of the bags and laid it on the ground. Carefully he held the top of the bag closed and at arm's length, as far from his body as he could hold it without letting go. Then he stomped on it. Over and over.

The rats inside screeched in panic their high-pitched squeals of pain. The bag came alive as they tried to flee. The man stomped and shook the bag, stomped on the bag and shook it again, and kept stomping until finally the bag was still. The man hung the bag up neatly again and took down the next bag. He shook it to see if there was still life inside. When the rats stirred, the man put the bag on the ground and stomped the second batch of rats dead.

The man looked up. There was no agitation in his face, no look of disgust at either having done what he had done nor at having had to do it. There was an expression in his eyes of an icy emptiness.

It was this look that I had seen so many times before— too many times before—in the eyes of other black men. It is the look in their eyes of insignificance, no matter how defiant their gestures, the look of not being taken seriously, the look of being ignored. It is the look of believing what they have been told about themselves. It is the look in their eyes of surrender.

I have known very well that look of surrender. I have seen something like it often enough in my own eyes. It too is a kind of submission, and it hides behind my own arrogance, my own defiance, but it is surrender nonetheless, a surrender of an even more noxious nature, perhaps, because it comes from the oddly unfortunate vantage point of good fortune. But in my own ways I too wear that look of surrender. It is the look in my eyes of believing what I have been told about them—not about myself, I tell myself, but about *them*—as if somehow I can remain apart from them and they are different from me, as if somehow I am not them.

Harlem is where they live, and where I have come, and where, of course, I can always leave. Or so I have told myself. After these two years of living here, however, I now am not so sure.

An old Italian man I vaguely know fled from his native Italy when he was a young man. The Fascists were on the rise. Italy was in the middle of a depression, as was the rest of the world. In those times life in a small village must have been pretty tough. And that is all I know of this man and his situation. He might have been escaping the troubles already existing in Europe or running from the war that was on its way. He might have been looking for a better way to live than what was offered where he had grown up. For all I know he might have simply wanted to expand his horizons. I don't know his circumstance, but I once called him a coward anyway; called him a coward because he did not stay in Italy to fight against the evil that was spreading across his land; called him a coward because he would not stay to fight and to make his homeland the better place he sought elsewhere.

If this is cowardice, then I too have been a coward. I left home the same as the old Italian. I left that area of my life that I now call Harlem and I almost never looked back, left all that was familiar to me and even comfortable, turned my back on family and friends and neighbors, if not in any absolute way then at least in a metaphorical way, and perhaps not consciously, but I left them just the same. I have been away ever since.

I have also, in a way, been homeless ever since.

I left on a Saturday afternoon. I was ten years old. My family had recently moved to the suburbs. And on this Saturday I was sent to get a haircut. I left the house, took a right turn, or perhaps a wrong turn, I may never know which, and left Harlem. In leaving this place, I was leaving behind a world that was all black. I never really went back there. I never even looked back—until now. Suddenly Harlem began to whisper in the ear of my imaginings. Harlem began to sing to me, to speak to me, to call me home.

So I returned to Harlem, even though I had never lived there—came back for the first time a little over two years ago, came back although in truth I had never been here before, came back although in a certain sense I had never been away.

Harlem is like that. For Blackamericans, there is in a way no escaping it, no leaving this place. Even if you have never been here before, you have always been here. As Ralph Ellison once said, *"Harlem goes where black folks go,"* and try as one might to get out from under it, the shadow of Harlem falls over us all.

For Harlem is the alabaster vessel that holds the Blackamerican heart, that holds the history and hope of Blackamerica, that holds as well its frustrations and its desperation, so much of the poverty of spirit, the bitter pain and isolation of being black, and so much too of the energy, vitality, and exuberance. Harlem carries on its back the psychological freight of a people and perhaps of an entire nation as well.

Harlem is music in the soul of a people, a rhapsody, a torch song, a love song, a child's incantation. Harlem is a lullaby whispered in the long long night, a blues song repeated endlessly and coming from a place so deep in the Blackamerican soul and psyche that the words and the music are somehow known long before you have heard them for the first time, and quite impossible to forget. They are ingrained in the Blackamerican subconscious and part of the Blackamerican idiom. Harlem is the metaphor for black America.

I decided that Saturday afternoon not to go to the barbershop where my father and brother always went, where the barbers were black and the old men who sat and laughed at my father's antics were black and so were the little boys who waited patiently for their turn and never spoke a word. Their legs dangled over the edges of chairs too high for their feet to touch the floor. In an effort to be like the big boys and like the men, they slouched and tried hard to keep at least a toe tipping the ground. They watched in silence as the older men joked or talked about events in the news or in the neighborhood. The little boys kept still. They were watching carefully and listening, learning how to be black men.

I wasn't so interested in being a black man, just a man. I had watched and had been scarred the previous year by the doings of three black men, Johnny Cannon and his partner and the man they both stabbed, and if this was part of what it meant to be a black man, then a black man was not the kind of man I wanted to be.

I went that day to the barbershop where there was no gaiety in getting a haircut. There was just a stern white barber and a few quiet white men reading old magazines, no loud talking, no boasting or bragging, no laughter until I walked in and quickly out again.

"We don't cut black hair in here," the white man said.

I had no idea what he meant. I was just a little boy.

"Mister," I said. "My hair is brown."

Probably they are laughing still, but the world they had inherited, the world they then adopted, adapted, and made their own before passing it on to their heirs, is now no laughing matter. The trickle has turned into a stream turned into a river turned into Niagara Falls. The men in that barbershop could not see or would not see what I, even as a ten-year-old, could see.

I knew their world was not the one I could entirely embrace either. I was and would for a long time be lost somewhere in the middle.

I cannot honestly say that I made up my mind right there and then about anything. I hated haircuts and had not wanted one in the first place. I'm sure it had been my mother's idea. Now I had an excuse and left that barbershop rather gleeful, if slightly confused. Certainly I did not feel humiliated; perhaps I should have. There were no defiant gestures; perhaps there should have been. I did not shout back, made no threats, never once pledged aloud or to myself, "As God is my witness——," or any such thing. Instead I went to play.

But even as I was out playing, I was refusing to be swept to the margins and off the page completely. Or better still, I was deciding, inasmuch as it is at all possible, to make my own tableau, give my tapestry its own design, shape, and texture. All the rest would be background and border.

Such notions sneak rather than spring into the minds of ten-year-old boys. Somehow in the intervening years, however, I woke up to discover I was clinging so hard to the center that I had separated from the margins, the way meringue not firmly held against the sides of the pie pan will pull away from the edges. It makes for an ugly lemon meringue pie, but it's still a pie.

A person, though, can think he or she is something altogether new, an island, perhaps, wholly apart from the exotic lands just off its shore but always in sight. But beneath the sea the lands are one. There is no escaping it.

I have spent more time now in exile than ever I spent in the world of black folk, that world I now refer to as Harlem. I don't know how much of my former self I left behind in that world. I wonder now how much of that world, hidden inside me, I carried out.

I lie awake mornings and ponder. Very often lately the words of a song that I haven't heard in a long time turn inside my head. A song that asks, when I sing it in my own voice, who am I, a song that has me wondering if I am a mere résumé and nothing more, a portrait in words.

Is that who I am, is that all I am, a listing of things I've done, places I've been, books I've read? If so, it paints a picture of someone I do not recognize. It does not tell me really who is this person that is me, what I think, what I feel, what I know. It cannot tell me what I am doing here.

I lie straight and still in my bed. I do not move. I make barely any noise. The rhythms I hear come from the steadiness of my breathing and from the sound of my heart beating hard against my ribs. I lie in bed and listen to the words running inside my head.

When I least expect it, a gunshot rings out to call me awake, to remind me, to rip open the stillness of an early morning and let me know that I am in a world I am not familiar with, a world quite possibly where I do not belong.

The rapid-fire crackle from a small-caliber pistol shouts good morning, greeting and warning at the same time, flying over the rooftops and entering the courtyard behind my apartment. Five sharp bangs cry out, explode, hit the walls and windows and echo into every direction off the pavement and the brick sides of the buildings. It is impossible to tell this morning where the shooting comes from. But then, it always is.

When I hear shots—and I often hear shots—it is usually at night, often in the late evening, but never at this time of day, never in the morning.

Early morning is the only still and peaceful part of the day in Harlem. I like to waken early—four-thirty, five o'clock—when the sky in summer is just beginning to glow and the gray just edging toward blue. I like to lie calm and quiet for a little while in my bed, to think and have little conversations in my head, and to listen to the silence. There is no noise as yet on the street. The shouting and the music that continue all day haven't yet begun, nor the police sirens, the car alarms, the delivery trucks. I lie in the half-light of dawn, in the conscious coma of almost awake, and I listen for the sounds escorting the new day. Morning slides open gradually—unless, of course, it is trash day. Trash trucks shatter the stillness even more abruptly than the gunshots.

When I hear gunshots—and I hear them very often lately, too often—I always think they come from the housing project at Amsterdam Avenue and 133rd Street. I don't know why. Something about the way the sound enters my apartment. Something too, I suppose, about the way I perceive big urban housing projects, desperately overcrowded and very dangerous; but the shots could have come just as easily from somewhere farther down the avenue, or from just around the corner on 133rd itself, or even from just down this block.

A car alarm somewhere nearby goes off. As usual, no one pays much attention.

I look out the window of my apartment, and far away in the southern distance Manhattan rises above Central Park. The park spreads out almost like an oasis, but more like a no-man's land. Beyond it lies an El Dorado where the streets are paved with gold. A land of milk and honey and money. Oz's Emerald City. Paradise. From here, that is how it sometimes seems.

On days when the air is clear and still, especially on stormy summer days when the rain has washed away smog and haze, when there is darkness in the deep distance and rain where I am, and yet the sky is clear near the park, there is a dreamy otherworld quality to the light and to the city it bathes. Light and dark, clouds and clear sky, all swirl together in chiaroscuro and bright blue. Patches of darkness shroud parts of the picture. Light falling in streams selectively illuminates the rest. The high-rise apartments of the Upper East Side and the office buildings of Midtown stand out as white as any Portuguese Algarve village gleaming in the bright light of the Mediterranean sun.

From here the rest of the world seems so unreal, shimmering almost like a mirage, so unaffected, so remote, and so removed. A world away. Another world entirely. A world that begins and ends—as this one does—at 110th Street. By formal definition greater Harlem spreads from river to river—from the Hudson to the East River—and runs from 90th Street to 178th Street; central Harlem, from 96th Street to 155th. But no matter how you define this neighborhood, you don't reach the heart of Harlem until you cross 110th Street. From there on you know you are in a different world. The moment you set foot onto 110th, you have entered into the fullness of Harlem.

It is, isn't it, the way we want things, clear frontiers and easy distinctions between here and there, between what is real and what isn't, between us and them. The lines, once drawn, however, no matter how thinly, no matter how broad, begin immediately to flex and then to blur. Shadows fall toward both sides, depending on the light, cultures spill and spread, and there is a subtle sameness for a distance on either side of any frontier.

And here am I, one of the border shadows that falls to either side but that never quite reaches the heart of this side or that one, that never reaches too far beyond this hazy ground in the middle.

To whom do I belong, to which of these two sides? In which culture and in which set of values do I claim citizenship? Whose passport do I carry and to whom is owed my allegiance?

These are questions that have no easy or clear-cut answers. The odd thing about them is that I was never plagued by them before. I rarely even considered them. Now, however, they cause so much turmoil within that the questions themselves, let alone any answers I might ever come up with, color my every action, my every thought. Nearly every question is draped in a black shroud.

Is the wider world available to me too that I may lay claim to it or if I am to care, must the things I care about be only those things that black people care about? And if I am to live, must I limit myself and my choices to those places we consider black places, restrict myself to life on a reservation because that is what has been reserved for me—and without anyone asking me—places like this one where I now find myself, precisely because of these questions, these wonderings, this sudden sense of being caught in the middle and not belonging anywhere?

I wonder, then, since this is the world chosen for me and not chosen by me—I wonder then not only if I belong here but if I can fit in here. Ought I to even try?

Over and over I tell myself that I am not a prisoner here. I realize of course that I am. I am a prisoner of this place.

That is how I feel, oddly, like a prisoner on parole who has been called back before the prison board and who must spend a night or two in the cell block before final decisions can be made.

Over and over I tell myself that I am not a prisoner here, that I can leave this place anytime I choose, and that my world is the much wider world beyond the borders of this neighborhood. Still in my heart I know that, as voluntary as my confinement here is, I am as trapped as anyone for whom this *is* the wider world, as trapped as those who have lived here and tried to escape, as trapped as those who will never find a way out. I am a prisoner of this racialist thinking.

There is, of course, no way out, for Harlem is more than a neighborhood, more too than merely metaphor. Harlem is a state of mind, in many ways like a very dark dungeon. Once you have experienced it, there can be no going back. You can leave this place, but you can never get away from it—no, not really. Once you have lived here in earnest, once Harlem gets into your psyche and into your blood, the way it has gotten into mine, then you will carry it with you wherever you go and for the rest of your life, not as some moveable feast, but perhaps as a moveable famine, a reminder not of life's great banquet but of the meager table life lays for paupers.

We who live beyond these borders may need from time to time to be reminded. We who live in places like Harlem can never truly forget. We cannot forget how discarded and forgotten we are.

We are all prisoners here, prisoners of this place and its history, prisoners of our own history—even as we set about to make it.

For many who don't live here this seems to be among the scariest of propositions, persuaded as they are by fantasies of darkness and crowded streets, of black men robbers, black men thieves, black men the dealers of dope, the users and the fiends. They have no other idea, nothing to rely on but the images they glean from the TV, rumor and hearsay and wild imaginings. They think that when they cross 110th Street, they will have stepped into the darkness, into what might very well be, in fact, the darkest, dirtiest, most dangerous place on this earth. They—the brave ones who actually do, and even the ones who make the crossing only in their minds—they cross 110th Street and enter a world swarming with their worst fantasies.

Such is the power of Harlem and its myth.

A woman on a hot late-summer day steps onto the A train at 42nd Street. A young white woman pushing a baby stroller; she is obviously an au pair, the baby not her own. She speaks with a European accent and is going somewhere on the Upper West Side of Manhattan. But after 59th Street the A train will not stop again until it reaches Harlem.

The woman translates the announcement in her head. You watch her eyes as she listens. You see the way her brow knits as she struggles first to hear and then to understand the crackly voice amid the noises of loud conversation, metal wheels scraping, doors sliding shut. You watch and you wait and then finally you see what you knew you would see: panic registering on her face, the recognition of her worst, most unhoped-for expectations. Harlem!

It is too late. The doors have closed. The train is moving. Next stop, 125th Street.

Over and over you can tell yourself that you are not a prisoner here. And people do. But in time you will realize that you are. You will know better than to think that anyone could live in a place like this and certainly not ponder it without being as profoundly affected as by time spent in prison, ever surrounded by high walls, bars and barbed wire. Without the walls, without gun turrets and guard towers, Harlem nevertheless is a prison.

If you look you can see a prison of poverty in the tired faces of the people you pass on the street, noble faces sagging and puffy, eyes dimmed or dimming from not enough chances, from not knowing which way if any is the right path to follow; young faces projecting strength and courage and very much posturing; older faces lined with an eternal frown from squinting in the sun, from scowling at the heaviness of a life that bends backs and turns walking into shuffling, faces furrowed from forever wondering why.

Time spent in Harlem is certainly no gentle sojourn in some provincial paradise, no cornucopia of riches and opportunity, no pleasurable garden of Eden. A year here for many would be more like a year in hell.

If you look you can see this aspect of the prison as well in the faces of those who are *not* trapped here. Whenever they chance to encounter this place, you see the look of panic that serves to further separate and isolate the prisoners on the inside from the prisoners on the outside.

I saw that look—which is panic, which is loathing, which is scorn, and which says, *I don't want to be here, bad things will happen to me here and I want to get out, I don't want to see this side of life, don't even want to know it exists, why in fact does it have to exist, and why must I encounter it?*—in the quivering bottom lip bitten almost until it bled and in the darting glances of the young white woman on the train that summer day two years ago. Wherever she was from, if she knew nothing else about Harlem, she was well aware of Harlem's dark shadows and that they are to be avoided. She seemed to know for certain that here was a place she did not want to find herself. She knew instinctively or at least had been told of Harlem's dangers, its poverty and its blackness, and that she had no business up there. When the train stopped at 125th Street, she picked up the stroller with the baby still in it and took the steps two at a time. She sprinted over to the opposite platform and leaped into the first train going back downtown.

This in part is what makes Harlem the prison it has become. Not many people on the outside want anything to do with the people on the inside.

To witness this extreme isolation can put a strain on the sensibilities of caring individuals. It can make you kind of sad. Or it can make you angry. Or quite simply, if you allow it to happen, it can make you open your eyes and wonder what's going on and why.

But there is another reaction that the white lady on the subway can elicit, an odd reaction perhaps, given the circumstance, or maybe not so odd, but it is the reaction I had, which made it very odd indeed. I hadn't yet moved to Harlem then. I was still only a visitor. I had come up that day to get the lie of the land, to get the feel of the place, and to continue the search for an apartment.

That search, by the way, had not been an easy one. I had been trying to find an apartment for weeks now, staying with friends who lived in the part of Manhattan called Chelsea and coming up to Harlem every day to find neighborhood newspapers like the *Amsterdam News* and to answer the ads

I found there. You don't find many ads for apartments in Harlem in any of the other newspapers in New York, as if to say people who read those other papers wouldn't be looking for apartments in Harlem, as if to say people from downtown are not thinking of moving that far uptown, as if to say the only people who would consider living in Harlem are already in Harlem, and they can find what they need in the local neighborhood papers.

The world of Harlem and the world farther south remain separate and distinct this way, far apart and well removed, only an eight-minute subway ride from one world to the other, from midtown Manhattan to Harlem, but nevertheless they are worlds apart, so far apart that the two worlds rarely even touch.

But their orbits this day passed in close proximity, if only for a moment. Their paths crossed. They almost came together. Then like a comet, the one world merely gained momentum from the gravitational pull of being so close to this other world that it spun away and zoomed out of sight. She picked up the baby carriage, hurled herself into the first train that stopped, and disappeared.

Normally, if someone is struggling up the stairs with a baby stroller, I will lean down, grab the front end of the thing, and together we will lift baby and stroller up the steps. No need to ask. No need to say a word. Bending over and reaching down says all that needs to be said. And the help is always appreciated.

But this time I made no such offer. This time I just watched, the same as I had been watching as she bit her lip and anxiously peered through the windows of the train and into the blackness of the subway tunnel. I'm sure she wanted to know where she was and how much farther she had to go before she could get off. She must have been trying to read the writing on the walls of each station we sped through. She made eye contact with no one. She looked at no one. She looked down at the floor or at the baby, or she looked through the windows. She had closed herself off in that urban cocoon wherein people—women especially—can appear to be looking right at you, but the gaze shifts somehow and it is as if they never even saw you, as if they were never looking at you at all.

When we had gotten to 125th Street and she had fled, when the downtown A train had slammed its doors around her, rattled off into the shaft that snakes underground, and taken her away to the safety of the Upper West Side, I threw my head back, opened my mouth wide, and let out a tremendous laugh.

The laughter was only in part derision at what I considered her foolishness and her prejudgments. She anyway could have taken her time to get to the downtown platform. She didn't really have to panic or be quite so nervous. It wasn't, after all, as if she had stumbled by mistake into a leper colony. But she acted as if all around her were more than mere contagion; here was a world where she did not belong, did not want to belong, wanted no part of. She wanted to be gone from Harlem as fast as speed could carry her.

I watched her and I made a silent cheer. *Be gone then*, I

speechlessly told her. *Be gone and get away from here. As much as you don't want to be here, we don't want you here. Go away from here, stay away from here, for this place, even if no other place on earth is, this place is ours.*

I had fallen into the trap. I identified with the *us* of this black world, as if I were and had always been a part of it.

Harlem is ours, I was telling myself. Harlem is *mine.*

I came up from the subway and into the bright light of day. I felt a little of what Langston Hughes must have felt when he first arrived in Harlem in 1922. It was a bright September afternoon that greeted me, a bright September afternoon that greeted him. And as he was happy and thrilled to be here, so was I, though probably not as much, for in 1922 Harlem was still young and new and its magic had yet to be tarnished. Langston Hughes was so delirious on coming here, he later wrote, that he was never able to capture on paper the excitement even of riding the subway uptown.

"I went up the steps," he said, *"and out into the bright September sunlight. Harlem! I stood there, dropped my bags, took a deep breath and felt happy again."*

I was happy to be here too. I turned the corner and was excited enough to leap up the stairs and go out, but instead I went slowly. At the bottom of the steps a man was folded against the wall and was sleeping there. I had to step over him before I could go up.

At the top of the steps an old woman, very thin and very shrunken, barred the exit and was begging for spare change.

When I climbed into the light, I took my own deep breath. The air all around the subway entrance smelled of urine.

Clearly this was not the Harlem of 1922.

Still, it was Harlem. Surely some of the old magic remained. And I was excited to be here, in touch at long last with what I had in many ways abandoned. I had come home again.

*T*he past is a dangerous place to visit. It offers itself as a safety zone. At the same time it is a place as treacherous as hell. It is beauty. It is also burden. It is where we go, many of us, to remind ourselves who we are, and even sometimes to find it out. It is where we go often when what is here and now begins to overwhelm us, when the present begins to tarnish, when it refuses to sparkle and glow. But if we are not careful there in the past, its hypnotic swirls can suck us into a vortex of irreality and disillusion.

I had been to the past many times before. My father used to take me there when I was a boy. He was looking, I think, for a world that no longer was—the past, *his* past, his former world that had in fact vanished a long time ago, a world that in his memory at least was somehow more everything: more fun, more difficult, harsher, softer, simpler, in a way more alive. Together we would search the scenes of his younger days, the places where he had played and gone to school, fought with the boys and toyed with the girls.

But the scenery by the time I got to it had all turned to

ashes and ruin. Nothing was as it had once been, of course; nothing ever is. All had crumbled away. You could see the changes washing across my father's face as we drove around the old neighborhood. The laughter from a long time ago that had been ringing in his ears began to fade. The smile he carried at the anticipation of going home again flattened out across his features into an expression bordering on sadness. His eyes had been sparkling like a child's. Now they dimmed a little. The wonder that had been in them was squeezed away in a wince of melancholic pain. The memories were within him still, but none of the people he knew were still living there. No one there knew him. There was no physical proof left that he had ever been there, or that he had quite simply ever been.

He looked at me as if I were his proof. He stared at me much too long with an expression like that of a deranged man or a demon. I have never liked that look. I knew what it meant.

He bit his lip. He shook his head. He asked me to pull up at the corner so he could step into the liquor store. In a little while he would be nearly drunk.

No! Nothing was the same, not on this trip into his past, not on the last one; nor would it be on the next one. Everything had changed, even the response to my father's particular brand of lunacy.

My father is a maniac. Not long ago this crazy man and I took a drive down to visit his sister Leola. She lives still in St. Louis, not very far in fact from the neighborhood where she and my father had been children. She has a nice house, kept up after all these years in a neighborhood that has deteriorated in time around her, and in her backyard there are fruit trees and a vegetable garden. She grows peaches and tomatoes that, while I'm upstairs visiting, my father likes to steal.

When we left my aunt's house we took a drive, as I knew we would, through the old neighborhood. This time, on the way out the smell of barbecue caught us in its grip and lured us with its enchantment. It defined our mission for the rest of the hour.

"Somewhere around here," my father said, "somebody's making our lunch. I think, I think, I think." He put his head out the window and started sniffing.

His smile was coming back.

We drove around awhile. Finally, on the corner of St. Louis Avenue and Newstead, in the derelict parking lot of a discount food store that had notices all over the windows shouting that food stamps were accepted, we found three women sitting in the shade of a makeshift canopy. They were bathing in the cloud of smoke that came from the huge metal barrel behind them that they had turned into the barbecue pit, and were fanning themselves.

As we drove past, my father eyed them carefully. Without turning toward me he said, "What do you think? Do you think it's all right?" Sometimes he can be quite squeamish about what he eats. Sometimes it seems he'll eat almost anything.

"It'll be all right," I said. "I'm hungry."

We parked the car up the street and walked back to the

corner. I walked not quite at his side, but a step or two behind him. I was the sidekick. I have always been the sidekick.

I have been this man's sidekick, in fact, since I was four years old and couldn't walk. I was born with a leg and foot deformity, and when I was four it was thought that surgery might correct the problem. During the long convalescence my father would throw me onto his shoulders and carry me wherever he went. We spent many hours together in Gracie's Tavern, on a corner not far from where we lived in those days.

It was a dimly lit place, if I remember correctly. In a corner there was a machine that was like a little bowling alley. My father would stand me up there and let me hurl the balls at those pretend bowling pins, which would retract violently when the ball hit the right spots on the table. Bells would ring, lights would flash, my father laughed. Then we would sit at the bar.

My father drank beer. I drank soda. I would sit on a stool next to him while he flirted with the barmaids or joked with the men. Every once in a while someone would say something to me. I was happy being my father's sidekick.

Since then we have traveled much together, this old man and I, though not as much as I would have liked. But then, he is not my friend the way he is friends with my brother Tommy. We don't share the same interests the way they do, don't talk about the same things. We are not alike at all, it seems, but more alike I suppose than I would ever have guessed. In fact one of the reasons I travel the way and as much as I do is that I learned it from my father. I am far better at it now than he ever was. I have shown him more in places he had been to without me than he ever saw on his own. In many ways he should be the sidekick, but he's not. He is still *the Man.*

He is now an eighty-year-old-plus man. He is to me still and has always been the embodiment of black manhood.

No, that's not quite right. He is the embodiment to me of manhood. When I grow up, I would like to be very much like him, although it can be argued that in a sense he has yet to grow up himself.

We sauntered to the corner, father and son, like two desperadoes in a Western. I stopped at the barbecue stand. My father didn't. He rounded the corner and looked over the scenery.

Many of the houses in the neighborhood looked as if they had been burned out and were boarded up. Most of them were empty. In the space between those houses, the yards were overgrown with weeds and debris. Where people still lived, the houses, the doors and windows, were protected with bars. Looking at this scene, I found it hard to tell if the bars were to keep people in or to keep people out, and just who, in fact, was the prisoner here. My father bit his lip and put on a face half sad, half sickened at the sight.

In the derelict parking lot, three men doing nothing leaned against the wall of the grocery shop. My father went to say something to them, probably about the demise of the old neighborhood, maybe to tell them how grand it once was here or to ask if anybody knew whatever happened to old Cootie Johnson who used to live on this corner, or what became of the tavern that used to be across the street. In a few minutes he had them all laughing. When he came back to where I stood trying to decide what to eat, he was wearing his big grin.

He said to the ladies sitting there, "All right now, baby. Give it up or show me where it is."

Nobody moved a muscle. Nobody knew what he was talking about. Knowing him as I do, I thought he was making some crude sexual innuendo—but again, knowing him as I do, he could have been speaking the language of a holdup man demanding the money or the safe where they hid it. Whatever he was saying, I laughed and he laughed. These three ladies were not in the least bit intimidated or amused, but clearly they didn't know what to make of this old man.

I didn't know what to make of him myself. I'm not sure I have ever known. But I watched with tremendous admiration as he glided into this world with the ease of a native well versed in its ways. The trouble was: these ladies didn't seem to be a part of the world he knew.

The world he knew was not an easy one, certainly. It was riddled with strife and with the struggle for justice and for fair treatment. In creating the world we now know, the larger society put restrictions on fairness, but none on hostility and resentfulness. My father has never been an idealist; he could never afford that comfort. Neither could he allow himself to surrender to the lure or to the luxury of defeat. He filled his world instead with the kind of laughter that made the bitterness bearable. A good time, he used to tell me, was always just a smile or a joke away.

"The white folks," he said, "have such petty concerns.

We get the monumental ones. That's why we laugh louder and party harder."

He speaks of a sense of unity that once existed, a sense of common struggle. Now, he says, it's every man for himself.

"It's always been like that," he tells me. "Every man for himself. Every *black* man for himself. Now there's something different about it. We used to like ourselves more. We used to like each other better. We used to have a certain lightness about us, and with all the evil shit going on around us, we knew how to enjoy who we were and what we had."

I watch my father, and he moves as if there is still that unity in blackness, still that enjoyment.

I looked around and I saw that the world my father knew was no more. Not that it mattered to him whether that world was gone or whether these women were a part of it; he carried that world with him always. He was who he was, and he was not going to try to be anything else.

It might have mattered to the women, though. They looked at him as if he were crazy.

When they had served us what we wanted, my father took his lunch away and went to talk to the men leaning against the wall by the grocery store. I watched him walk away. He is indeed an old man now, but he looks twenty years younger. And he acts it.

I spoke to the women.

"Don't mind him," I said. "He just remembers a time when being black was fun—a lot of fun."

I look at this old man who is my father and watch him negotiate his way into this world that I am no longer familiar with. I don't know how familiar with it he still is, since all of the world he knew has changed, but he glides effortlessly here. He seems to know these people, he speaks their language, and they seem to know him as one of their own. He talked to the men in the parking lot for over half an hour.

How much am I merely my father's son, and how much again am I actually my father? When these people see me, do they see the father in the son, do they see the father's world and his experience in my face, in my being and in my bearing? Or am I just the pussycat to the panther, related but not at all a part of this world, not at all belonging to it? Do they look at me and see something familiar, look at me and say, as they say in the South, "I know your people"? Do they see one of their own in me? And am I still in fact, after all this time away, one of their own, and can I make it here?

I get a headache when I try to sort it all out, but these are the questions that drove me to want to live in Harlem— to find out not so much who I am, for I think I know the answer to that one, but where exactly, if anywhere, I might fit in. Who are my people, and about whom should I care the most?

And is in fact any of this really mine?

I watch my father and I am reminded of and I see all that is beautiful about being black and about being a man and about being, I guess, a black man. Despite my protestations about not wanting to be seen as anything more or less than just a man, I *am* a black man—whatever that means—for I am a man and I am definitely black. Or so says the mirror.

I am a black man, say the people who see me, and in large measure we are or we become who other people tell us we are. We are what we are seen to be. We are what we allow ourselves to be treated as. We come to fit, we sanction and give credence to, most of us, the realities we let others create for us.

A distressing letter came for me the other day. A dear friend, Colin Schmidt in Tulsa, Oklahoma, wrote to me and relayed a bit of conversation he overheard his wife having with his daughter. The conversation was about me.

Colin is a white man. He is married to a white woman. She had previously been married to a black man and had two children with him before the divorce and her remarriage. Colin has been trying to raise those two black children as his own. He has been more of a father to them than the black man whose blood courses through their veins, but he is constantly aware of that blood as he has tried to shepherd these two daughters through the maze that is the struggle for racial identity. It is no easy task there in Tulsa, Oklahoma. Tulsa is not quite the bastion of diversity and tolerance and liberal thinking that it pretends to be.

I visited them once in order to lend something of a black male presence to the house. There aren't many black people where they live, and I was the first black *man*, I think, to set foot inside their home.

After my weekend there, so the letter says, the evening of the day I left, in fact, one daughter said something to her mom about me and black men in general. The mom and the elder daughter echoed the same sentiment. The mom replied, "Most black men are not like Eddy Harris."

I don't know what that means, but reading the letter puts me in mind of another friend, Jonathan Hunt, who lives in London and who once said to me, quite innocently, "Eddy, you are the whitest black man I have ever known."

Who makes these rules about what a black man is or is supposed to be, and why the narrow definition of acceptable blackness?

You are, I suppose, what you think and what you do and what you try to do. I am, so the mirror tells me and so the world that doesn't know me tells me, a black man. Therefore aren't the things I do and think and try the things that black men do, since I am a black man—and like all black men, never just a man?

40

Because I *am* a black man, because of the rules of the larger culture in which I am trapped, I am required to be like all the others who share my shade. Yet in this same culture we do not seem to expect all white folks to think and act white, nor any of the others, however we define them— race, family, neighborhood, right down to shoe size. We do not require that they act and think as the others in their community.

The world looks at me and already in an instant has decided who I am, who I will be, and how I will act. The world thinks it knows me.

That is possibly too simplistic. Maybe the things I do are not the things that black men do, although I do them and I am a black man. Maybe they are not the things black men are supposed to do. Maybe they are not the things black men are generally allowed to do. I don't know who made these rules either, but maybe the things I do are things, in fact, that black men do not want to do and absolutely must not do if they are to be real black men. Perhaps, then, I am not a black man—just a man after all, and the things I do are only those things that Eddy L. does, nothing more and nothing less.

According to the rules, I don't look mean enough to be a black man, don't act rough enough, don't talk tough enough. I am too soft to be a black man, an aesthete, a dandy, a man who wears white silk trousers, in a world where, one would imagine, white silk trousers are unheard of—the world of Harlem, that is.

I don't wear oversize basketball shoes and baggy pants, don't put my hats on backward. I don't talk loud unless I'm in an animated argument. I don't scowl unless the sun shines in my eyes. I don't demand respect; I just get it.

The French have an expression, *D'être bien dans sa peau*—to be at ease inside one's skin. My father is at ease, I believe, inside his skin. I am at ease inside my own. I am my father's child.

But am I, too, Harlem's child?

Things are a little different now than they were—certainly thirty, forty, seventy years ago when Harlem, as they say, was really Harlem. It is a long way from those old days to these days, just as it is from midtown Manhattan to Harlem: only an eight-minute ride, but still a world away; only a few years gone, but still a million miles from what it used to be. And remarkably, perhaps sadly, not yet far enough from where it used to be.

From that day when I first strode 125th Street like I owned the place, like I belonged there, and like I knew where I was going and what I was doing there; from that first day two years ago to my last day in Harlem and to the many days in between, things are a little different than they were.

Hundred and Twenty-fifth Street is Harlem's aorta. Perhaps it is only a throwback to an earlier era in Harlem, and perhaps 125th Street has always been this way, a visible testament to the life and vibrancy that has coursed through the now mean streets of this neighborhood for as long as Harlem has been black. Hundred and Twenty-fifth Street is evidence that there is still vibrant life in Harlem, and when you walk down this street you know it, you see it, you hear it, you feel it pulsating off walls, windows, and pavements. Or maybe 125th Street is a throwback all the way to Africa, for Africa is what it initially brings to mind. Hundred and Twenty-fifth Street is alive with confusion and commerce, noise and commotion and a hell of a lot of energy. It was even more alive that day, my first day in Harlem. Since then things have changed a little. Since then the police have moved in following orders from city hall, and they have curtailed much of the curbside hustle and bustle.

"It's what they do, man. It's what they always do. They don't care a shit about us until it's vote-getting time, and then the only ones they care about are the ones they can count, or the ones who can give them money, or the ones who look like they're on their same side. But the rest of us, you know, the ones of us who are out here struggling every day, trying our best to make it—man, we just get shit on. Especially if we are trying to buy into that American Dream stupidness."

That was the angry voice of Eliot Winston. I would not meet him until much later, and if his words were not this day ringing somehow in my ears as I strolled 125th Street for the first time, then this day would in my mind's eye replay itself later on when I walked with Eliot the day the changes to 125th Street were imposed. On that day, cordons of uniformed police were stationed all along the street. In twos and threes they stood outside the shops. Blue police barricades lined the curbs. Order and, some would say, boredom replaced 125th Street's normal chaos. Hundred and Twenty-fifth Street suddenly became a little more like any other street in New York, or in America—just a little blacker.

But on this day, my first day, 125th Street was still the old 125th Street.

I came up from the subway. I let the sun hit me, sit on my shoulders and face, let the sun darken me just a little blacker than I already was. I took a little survey, took a little breath, then I stepped off the curb and into the swelling sea of blackness.

Harlem. I was in it now. I was home.

At a publishing party in London, when the notion of living in Harlem was just occurring to me and taking shape, I had a conversation that addressed my chances of surviving Harlem. I was kicking the idea around in my own head to see how it fit, but tossing it around to others as if it were an idea already set in concrete. After all, following Africa and the Deep South, Harlem seemed like the next logical place for me to spend time.

I was overheard saying that I planned to live a year in Harlem—so I thought at the time, only a year—and that I planned to write about the experience. The woman I was talking to was appropriately impressed. She, I am told, registered something like a look of shock, no doubt projecting herself into my shoes and wondering how Harlem might be for her and whether *she* could survive it—as if Harlem were some kind of war zone.

"Do you think you'll be all right there?" she wanted to know. "Do you think you'll be safe?"

She is small, this woman, and white. She could see the

world only through those delicate blue eyes of hers. I see the world through the eyes of a man who is black and who is tall and who, when he frowns and stands erect, making himself appear somehow larger, like a grizzly bear rearing up on hind legs, projects a formidable image, belied most of the time by kind watery eyes and a smile that turns his face into a baby's face. I am a coward, I am sure, but I am able to live and move within the bubble of certainty that not many people would take the risk implied by the image of me. I knew I'd be safe. And I told her so.

Safety never occurred to me before, nor very often during my time in Harlem. There would be over the course of the two years a few close calls, a few scrapes to call into question the ease and confidence with which I came to move in Harlem. I had been shot at, of course. I had stepped into a few tight spots and found myself in an altercation or two. And before it was all over, there would be, in the street right below my window, a man beating a woman. I had, however, the physical passport always to protect me.

I was not small, I was not frail, I do not look like anybody's victim. And more than that, I am black. If nothing else, on first glance anyway, I look like I belong here. *These are my people,* I kept telling myself. *I'll be at home here.*

But Joseph Carver, who used to live in Harlem, reminded me not to wade too deep into the quicksand of racial identification. He warned me that it would be best not to be too foolish, not to let my guard down completely.

"Black people do some pretty bad things to other black people," he said one afternoon over a shared pizza. He had lived in Harlem and his apartment had been broken into too many times.

"It got so bad," he said, "I couldn't leave without worrying about somebody stealing my stuff. So you either worry all the time or you get used to living without having anything. I didn't want to live the one way or the other. So I left."

And then, as if to emphasize, he told me the story of Bill Simpson, a thirty-seven-year-old black man who the previous winter had moved to Vidor, in east Texas. It was a story Joseph had read in the paper or seen on TV.

The federal housing projects in that part of Texas where Simpson lived were highly segregated, and Simpson's move was part of a court-ordered integration plan. He was one of only two blacks in his new town, which had been all white before the court order, and he was constantly harassed, he said, because of his race, and constantly on edge. He was all but ready to move back to Beaumont, where he had lived before moving to Vidor, to be back among his people.

"I don't want to worry who's going to do something and what they're going to do, when it's going to happen, where it's going to happen," he once said.

So on a Wednesday afternoon he moved back to Beaumont, Texas.

Wednesday night, he was dead.

He had been shot five times as he walked along a street in Beaumont. A car had pulled up, the four men inside the car had demanded money. Simpson refused. One of the robbers shot him. The gunman was black.

Joseph Carver said, "Just because you're black, you can't think you're safe here or anyplace else. You can't think somebody's not out to hurt you. Especially if you've got more than he's got or if you've got something he wants. And you don't even have to. You just have to look like you do."

I think I heard myself say, and I'm not sure if I said it to Joe or if I was only saying it to myself: Perhaps I ought to be very afraid here.

But I'm not!

I knew right then that there was no place on earth I would rather be.

I knew I needed to be here.

I felt like an orphan reunited with the parents he has not seen since a very long time ago. I felt like my father back once more in the old neighborhood. Elation blended with trepidation, relief commingled with tension, producing in me an intense desire to laugh, to shout, even to dance with the dancing man who stands on a cardboard mat on 125th Street between Frederick Douglass and Adam Clayton Powell Jr.—what used to be, before all the name changes, Eighth Avenue and Seventh Avenue. He stands in the shadow of the Apollo Theatre, and instead of begging for money, he dances for tips. If donations from passersby are not forthcoming, he dances there anyway.

I stopped a minute or two and watched him. He wore a pair of reddish brown boots highly polished to catch the light of the sun. They shone so brightly that the red in them overtook the brown and they shimmered like fire. From every angle his boots threw light into your eyes. He wore a beret, loose black trousers, sunglasses, a string of shells around his neck. He stayed on the cardboard mat and danced, moving very slowly, almost carefully. He seemed unaware of the people who passed. He seemed to dance only for the fun of it, the sheer pleasure of hearing the music and feeling the movement of his body. But if you watched his face and not the dancing, you could catch a glimpse behind the sunglasses and you would see every now and again that he glanced up and took notice from the corner of his eye.

I smiled at him, but he never acknowledged me. He was in his own world, completely within himself—or at least pretending to be. I left him there and walked on, deeper into the tunnel of darkness, a little further back in time and into a world where is written clearly the history of modern black America—which is of course the history, quite simply, of modern America.

As I walked the streets that day, my first day in Harlem, I could feel that history—not just on 125th Street but throughout the district. It was like walking through a living museum where someone pushes a button and you hear recordings of sounds and voices and see images of times gone by.

I felt that I was walking among the ghosts of Harlem's past, that I was coming here as they had come here, as Langston Hughes had come and Duke Ellington had come, as they all had come: the washerwoman and the seamstress; the heiress and the showgirl; the hard-laboring man and the vagrant; the high and mighty, the lowly and disregarded; the leaders and the followers; artists and intellectuals— coming home, coming to find peace, coming to gain in Harlem a sense of self and a new way of defining oneself, blackness, black culture, black awareness, that was independent of the white world's limiting influence and strictures and prying eyes. Here they and we and I could live completely within ourselves, in a world all black, all our own and of our own making. Or at least, like the dancing man, we could pretend to.

I felt the weight of Harlem's hope and the rhythms of its excitement. They were all around me, in my ears and in my eyes and upon my shoulders. They stirred in my soul like some half-forgotten memory now suddenly awakened. I felt amazingly free, as if I were really and truly free for the very first time in my life.

At the same time I felt strangely burdened, about as unfree and bound as anyone could be. I felt somehow as if I owed somebody something.

By 1925 Harlem was already the center of a certain universe, spinning in an orbit all its own, attracting other worlds to itself with the gravitational pull of an immense black hole. The August issue of the *Saturday Evening Post* that year noted that Harlem was drawing immigrants "from every country in the world that has a colored population. Ambitious and talented colored youth on every continent look forward to reaching Harlem. It is the Mecca for all those who seek Opportunity with a capital *O.*"

James Weldon Johnson came to Harlem from Florida, Marcus Garvey and Claude McKay came from Jamaica. W. E. B. Du Bois came from New England, Langston Hughes came from Kansas.

They came to Harlem from everywhere; people whose names should be on the tip of your tongue, people you never

ever heard of. Businessmen came and racketeers came, profiteers and preachers came, the honest and the fakers. Nella Larson came. Madame C. J. Walker came. Pig Foot Mary came.

These came as they all came: seeking better. Some sought fame, some sought fortune, and some sought only the future. All of them sought the freedom that could not be had anywhere but here.

They came to Harlem the same as I had come: because Harlem seemed the place to be, the place where you could lose yourself and at the same time find yourself.

Harlem by then had already become more than a place. It was becoming the metaphor. It was becoming the fiery hot liquid center of black creation, the supernova core of a galaxy in the making.

For the outside world Harlem was quickly setting the tone of the time, those energetic Jazz Age years when the war to end all wars was over and the Great Depression had not yet begun. It was a time of enormous excess. Life seemed good and was getting better all the time, but after such a war you could never be sure. Better to live for the moment. For those who did, Harlem was nightclubs and liquor and music. For those with a deeper vision, Harlem was the creative spirit of an era. Here, in terms of art and music and literature, was Paris and Berlin of the same era rolled into one, but with one tremendous difference. Here at last were the as yet unknown and unheard voices, not of a generation, however lost and suddenly found, but of an entire people stumbling on untested legs and falteringly learning to walk, squeaking and squawking to find a voice and then to find something to say.

And I was walking among their ghosts. I felt indeed as if I owed them something.

This was Harlem in those long-gone days. It was more than the place to be, it was the place you *had* to be if you were black, the place that called you and where your heart was, even if you never set foot there. It was a movement at the center of which was the search for a place of equality in American society, equality based on pride and what W.E.B. Du Bois called uplift. Harlem was the seat of the black search for an artistic and intellectual self, the search for identity that emerged during what we now label the Harlem Renaissance, the emergence of black culture to find its soul.

Blackamerica's mission in creating the center of its universe in Harlem was not only to build a black city, a mere place. Its purpose was to make possible this search for a new identity. As Alain Locke once said so plainly, "Negro life is not only establishing new contacts and founding new centers, it is finding a new soul."

And so they came to find it or to forge it—a new black identity.

It was the reason Langston Hughes was drawn here. "Harlem," he said, "was like a great magnet for the Negro intellectual, pulling him from everywhere."

It was the reason Claude McKay found himself here. He came to achieve, he said, "something new, something in the spirit and accent of America."

They came all of them with the best of intentions. They came to participate. They came to contribute to Harlem's growing glory and to benefit from it. What no one considered, however, and what no one realized at the time was that they all came sowing the seeds of Harlem's very destruction—and perhaps all of Blackamerica's as well.

I too ignored those seeds of destruction already sown, already taken root, already sprouted. In my eagerness to be in Harlem, to find or maybe to forge a new black identity of my own, I could feel the weight only of Harlem's former glory and of its former hope and promise.

It is promise of a bygone era, promise that by now perhaps has been denied, promise that perhaps has faded, but from the vantage point of 125th Street that day, it was promise only that had been altered and that had shifted but that had not yet died. Hundred and Twenty-fifth Street was alive. Harlem was alive.

They were just as alive that day—Harlem and 125th Street—as they had been in 1923 when Duke Ellington first came here; differently alive, to be sure, but alive and throbbing with pace and excitement. The Duke is said to have practically roared with enthusiasm. He said of Harlem that here was the world's most glamorous atmosphere, exclaiming at the time, "Why, it's just like the Arabian Nights."

I don't know about the Arabian Nights or about the streets being particularly glamorous, but the excitement, the pace, and the noise were undeniable.

On this day, as on every day except Sunday, Saturdays being the worst, from St. Nicholas Avenue right the way across to Third Avenue, 125th Street was clogged with traffic. Cars and buses sped whenever possible, inched along most of the time, and drivers took out their frustrations in a symphony of horn honking that was mostly ignored except by those wishing to honk back. The effect was negligible on the movement of traffic but very great on the ear until you got used to it. Then the horn noise and traffic noise merged with the other sounds of 125th Street—the music blaring, the laughter rising above the streets, the children crying for one more piece of candy, one more hot dog, one more minute to look at something—and helped to carry you along. And you needed every aid, for the pedestrian traffic on the sidewalk was every bit as intense as the car and bus traffic in the street.

From practically one end of the street to the other, on both sides of the street, 125th was jammed tight with shoppers and strollers and people just standing, looking, and listening. Soapbox orators drew crowds on one corner or another as preachers and prophets railed against the wages of sin, urged you to seek Jesus or Allah, or simply attacked the white man and his ways. Street vendors sold on folding tables everything from souvenir T-shirts to compact discs and videocassettes, to books and barbecued chicken. As you walk you are bombarded every few steps by examples of the music for sale, first jazz then reggae then rap, all of it blasted at megavolume so you are sure not to miss any of it, and trying to compete with the loud music are the voices of the vendors shouting at you, trying to draw your attention to this table of books or that table of incense and crystals, photographs, paintings, clothes. It is noisy and hectic, and anyone trying to walk in a hurry along the street is just out of luck. And anyone trying to enter any of the shops on 125th Street needs extra determination, for to try and cut across the current of this mighty river of people moving first one way and then the other along the sidewalk is like trying to canoe upstream on the Old Man Mississippi River itself. It's no wonder the shopkeepers here constantly complained about the street vendors. It was enough trouble just getting inside the shops. What's more, the street vendors sold much of the same material and, without the overhead of the shopkeepers, at much lower prices.

Baseball caps for sale, blue jeans and cassette tapes, sheets, towels, and socks, games and candy: all from boxes carried or set on the pavement or from the folding tables that line the curb.

On the corner of Malcolm X Boulevard—what used to be Lenox Avenue—the vendors crowd together in what looks and feels and even sounds and smells like a market anywhere in West Africa. They sell much of the same things in much the same kind of chaos, African trinkets and African cloth, and in fact many of the vendors have come from Africa, drawn to Harlem by many of the same things that motivated earlier generations to come here from Africa, from Jamaica, from the Deep South.

I can't help but think of Harlem in an earlier time when I walk these streets, can't help but see in these faces the faces of a generation for whom Harlem was the way up and out of the mire of blackness and into the glory of being black.

When I look at the woman called Khakira, I think of a

woman my father used to talk about. She lived in Harlem in the 1920s and went by the name Pig Foot Mary. She had come to Harlem with practically nothing. She sold her wares on the streets of Harlem just as Khakira does, and by 1925 she was worth almost half a million dollars.

Khakira has her gimmick, just as Pig Foot Mary had hers, just as all the vendors do, selling, as they all do, whether they know the story or not, what they hope will help them to repeat Pig Foot Mary's rags-to-riches success.

Khakira wears floppy hats and clothes that come from Africa. Depending on what you sell, it is often best to appeal here to an Afrocentric consciousness and at the very least to show some sense of solidarity with black Africa, for here is where black Africa and black America meet. But Khakira, when she talks, sounds like she could be from almost anywhere, the Caribbean, North Carolina, Brooklyn. She sells incense and is known on 125th Street as the woman who smokes cigars.

A man called Ahmed speaks very little English. He really does come from Africa, from Mali, he says, as do most of the things he sells, the trinkets, the medallions, the pieces of carved metal shaped like the continent of Africa.

There are fertility necklaces on sale here, bean pies, African clothing. And here at the junction of black Africa and black America you can buy sweet potato pies and Malcolm X potato chips, assorted hats, assorted black nationalist tracts, books on the blackness of Jesus, books about a Blackamerican man traveling in Africa. Among the smells of sausages frying are mingled the smells of Jamaican jerk chicken and somebody cooking barbecue. And everybody,

everybody jammed tight shoulder to shoulder in what seems to be a never-ending swell of blackness as far as the eye can see.

Here on 125th Street you can find it all, most of it legal, some of it not. It is, all of it, the same grasping for dollars— the only true yardstick in America—that you find in any of the shops along 125th or along Madison Avenue or Fifth Avenue or any other shop on any other street. But here, the grasping has a decidedly black and African aspect to it that renders it more colorful than anything else.

Black or white or any other color, the aim is still the same though.

I turned the corner and walked up Malcolm X/Lenox Avenue. I stopped for lunch at Sylvia's, a famous soul food restaurant a couple of blocks up, and ate a meal straight out of my childhood: the tenderest spare ribs ever, collard greens, candied yams, black-eyed peas, and sweet potato pie. Then I continued my walk up to 135th Street for no other reason than to be on the corner where Pig Foot Mary made her fortune.

I think of her as Harlem's patron saint perhaps, for she in a way comes to symbolize for me, more than Duke Ellington, more than Langston Hughes, more than all the rest, the Harlem that many if not most people who came here were seeking: Harlem, the land of opportunity. Hers is the kind of story that would have become myth even as she was living it, and that needs to be remembered.

My father would tell the story as if Pig Foot Mary were a distant family relation. Her name was Lillian Harris. She was born in that part of Mississippi known as the Delta. My father's family comes out of Tennessee, but that part of Tennessee is only a puddle jump from the Mississippi Delta. For all I know she might very well have been a relative. Knowing my father as I do, he might just as easily have been making up the whole story. In this case, however, he didn't.

Pig Foot Mary, even more than the radiant luminaries of the Harlem Renaissance, exemplifies to me what the Harlem of old was very much all about.

She was born in 1870 and left Mississippi when she was a young adult, still a teen really, and headed north. She was doing no more, perhaps, than many other black southerners escaping to the North and East. Pig Foot Mary was one of them, fleeing, in what some might consider an act of cowardice, the tyranny and terror and hopelessness of the South when her talents and determination might have served as a better example had she remained where she was. Or perhaps in trying to make a better life for herself she was exuding, others might say, the same sense of bravery and pioneer spirit for which we tend to honor the frontier men and women who subjugated the American West, and for which we need to honor the pioneers who came to Harlem, for theirs was the very same intention, that of forging a new life in a better place and of finding possibility where none might otherwise exist.

Pig Foot Mary left home with nothing, for presumably in the Mississippi Delta she would have had nothing, or at best very little. She reportedly tried her luck for over ten years in several northern cities before hitching rides on hay wagons, milk wagons, and vegetable carts, finally reaching New York City in 1901. She had five dollars in her pocket.

With these five dollars, Pig Foot Mary went into business.

With three of these dollars she bought an old baby carriage and a small boiler. With the rest she gambled, bought two dollars' worth of pig feet, and turned that old baby carriage and boiler into a traveling restaurant.

To start with, she sold boiled pig feet to those of her countrymen who longed for the flavors of "down home." There were so many homesick southern blacks in Harlem that in no time business was thriving enough that she could expand the menu to include still more southern fare: chitterlings, hog maw, steamed corn, and always, always, the pig feet—cheap southern food that had yet to achieve cuisine status.

In a month's time the business was booming. In 1917 she had moved to the corner of Lenox and 135th Street, acquired a husband and a prosperous newsstand, and soon started investing in real estate. Eight years later, she who had once scraped by in a small one-room apartment was worth half a million dollars.

Then, success story complete, I suppose, she moved out of Harlem and went to live in Pasadena, California.

A twinge of something, I don't know what, touched the back of my heart all of a sudden as I stood there then. It was the same dull ache that day on the corner of 135th Street and Seventh Avenue as the pang that would nag at me that night, that early morning more than two years later when I would stand at the window of my apartment, look out to the street below, and spy on a black man as he tried to beat a black woman into submission. I cannot say if what I felt these two times—on this corner and at that window—was what I felt so many years before when I watched one black man stab another black man, for I cannot precisely remember the sensations I had on that distant day, but I imagine these feelings are all somewhat the same; and if not the same, at least related.

I would like to think that each of them represented somehow a moment of clarity, perhaps pieces of a grander moment of clarity, but I know nothing came anywhere close to clear until much much later.

I was encountering feelings similar to what an orphan

might have on meeting his birth parents for the first time since they gave him over for adoption; or better, like the prodigal son returning home having once taken that of his heritage which he found useful and then, casting aside all else, running away: that sense of belonging and not belonging at one and the same time.

I was indeed Harlem's prodigal son. I had taken my heritage, the parts I found useful, and had run away with it. I had chosen to live far away from home, far away from here, and squandered that birthright, some might say, while at the same time using it to my great advantage. By pulling myself out of Harlem, out of the world of blackness, I had done more than run away from home, away from this world; I had in fact abandoned it.

Here the elation blending with trepidation, and the relief commingling with tension, join with still another emotion even more powerful: guilt—and the questions that come with it. What might (here the ego speaks) this world have been had I remained in it? And what might I have been if I had stayed?

This last is the one that scares me.

I know now why these questions came rising from the corner of 135th Street and Seventh Avenue. This corner is my spiritual home. Pig Foot Mary, as much as she ought to be Harlem's patron saint, could very easily be my own personal patron.

Pig Foot Mary made her fortune here in Harlem. The foundation may have been laid elsewhere, but here on this very corner, on the site of an old newsstand, the walls went up. In the best sense of the word *exploit*, Pig Foot Mary exploited her resources, her drive, her ambition, her imagination, and her vision. At the same time—and here is where the word *exploit* turns a bit shady, and here I might be stretching things a little too far in trying to make a point—she exploited the very black people she had once served. She used them of course to make her fortune. She knew what they wanted and gave it to them. She took their trade. She took their money. It's only fair. But then, having come to Harlem, having exploited Harlem to the fullest measure, having become one of the wealthiest women in Harlem, she turned her back on the place and on the people. She got what she wanted and left the rest. She too, some might say, abandoned it.

She did not, however, turn her back completely. She had invested heavily in Harlem real estate, and although she no longer lived in the community, this community continued to support her. She became a wealthy absentee landlord, as unfeeling, it turns out, as any other. She was resolutely unsentimental about the condition out of which she had risen and unsympathetic about the plight in which many of her tenants still existed. Business being business, she cared, it seemed, not a whit for them or their circumstance. When the rent was slow in coming, she would write to her tenants, "Send it, and send it damn quick."

She continued to profit from the black community, but who could blame her—either for the profiting or for the leaving? Who could blame her for wanting to spend her old age in quiet and respectable retirement, tasting the sweeter side of life, the sunnier side far away from the desperate poverty and the dangers of Harlem's slums?

Harlem was the promised land, it is true. Harlem held out to black men and women the promise of a world made in their own image, a world of black self-respect and possibilities unknown to them elsewhere. But for the average dweller of this neighborhood, this world was still unkind and very difficult. Harlem was still a ghetto, and much of it was a slum, crowded and dirty.

As I stood on the corner of 135th Street and Seventh Avenue, I was planning, perhaps without knowing it, my own getaway, my own profit-taking.

I felt the weight of Harlem's history heavy upon my shoulders. I was thrilled to be here and dazzled by the radiance of the Harlem sun. Surely I was just a little bit blinded by it, as blinded as were they who came here dreaming of the glory of Harlem and brimming with hope, striving for a self-determination, self-awareness, and black identity that had not existed before, and which they found, many of them; and yet they were, as in my own way I was, planting without knowing it the seeds of the wasteland.

The wasteland has already been sown, already taken root, already sprouted. And I have helped to plant it. I ask myself again: what might this place have been had I, had Pig Foot Mary, had we all stayed?

I knew I would be in Harlem only for this short time and then gone. I did not come here to stay. This is not my world. I don't even know if I can pretend it is.

This world is the narrow world of Johnny Cannon doing his stabbing, the world of the man outside my window doing his beating. Although I was witness to both of these events, it is not a world I intimately know. I don't know it now that I have become this other thing.

This other thing that I have become is partly the fault of my mother, who when I started learning French in school began to call me her little Frenchman, and of my maniac father, who when I was young would joke by telling us that we were Jewish, Harris being, he said, a Jewish name. I didn't know he was joking. Sam the Tailor to whom we took our clothes to be mended was a Jew. His last name was Harris. Why not then my father, whose name likewise is Sam Harris?

I knew I was Catholic, of course. I never missed a Sunday Mass. But no one ever told me you couldn't be both Catholic and Jew. Or anything else, for that matter. My father also claimed that somewhere in his family someone was Chinese. My mother speaks of ancestors who came from Cuba.

From this bit of lunacy I figured I could define myself in any of several ways. I could be Jewish if I wanted to, no matter what the Jews say who define Jewishness not by what someone does to keep the faith, not by cultural or religious habits, but by the Jewish ancestry of one's mother. It's just a rule decided on. Stir up the Eddy Harris pot and you're likely to find almost anything. Other people's rules notwithstanding, I could define myself any way I pleased.

I admit I don't really know what it means to be one thing or another—black, Jewish, French. I doubt if anyone else does either. But someone is out there making the rules that stop us from being individuals and instead force us into groups, rules that steal away liberty and choice and shrink the realm of possibility.

Let me be free to choose: neighborhood, region, religion, taste in food. Let me honor the gods and cultures of my choice.

Culture—a word, a concept, that is tossed around much these days but never really defined. I have, of course, my own definition: that which people do to help them get through the day, and which in doing as a group tends to define the group.

But does following the practices of a particular group make you one of the group? The tribal chief in an Inupiak village might say no. I would ask rather, Why not?

With cheese and red wine I can become a little bit French. Seder supper on Passover, and I become a little bit Jewish. Why not?

I have been Irish on St. Patrick's Day, I eat pasta twice a week, I have an ongoing love affair with Mexico. Who was there to tell the small boy in me that I couldn't participate?

The world is mine, I thought as a young boy. Its cultures can all be mine.

Since I was a small boy playing at make-believe, I have put myself into the shoes of many men and women. I have lived in my head a life of others. I have been at times a soldier fighting Indians on the American frontier, and then turned around to be a Plains Indian fighting against those same soldiers and against the theft of my land. From the books I read when I was a young invalid, I became black man white woman Asian African Eskimo.

I have lived under the mistaken belief all these years

that this was what it meant to be truly American, that not only could I celebrate these cultures and these peoples but that I could somehow be them; that what they shared, I could share in as well, that I could be simply *citizen*, and by this one word so define myself: citizen first of country, citizen then of the wider world.

I never forgot that I was black, of course. Being black needed neither reminder nor effort but was evident each time I looked into the mirror, each time I sat down at the table with my family, each time my brother turned on the radio. Black culture surrounded us warmly and held the other cultures in place. Black culture was always there. It tethered us; we could—and would—always come back to that. In the meantime I grew up believing I could be anything or anyone I chose, and that I could do anything. I thought I could have it all, that I could be black and at the same time be more than just black. I have always wanted to be more.

I have never wanted to be limited.

But now I have come back—come back to limit myself—back to this culture, to this community, back to Harlem. But I have come back from a long way off, from such a long time gone in fact that Harlem is hardly mine anymore, hardly home now. I don't know if I belong here, if I can possibly fit here.

This was the worry, I think, of Clare Alexander, the woman in London who worried that skin color might not be enough, that size and stature might keep me safe but that safety might not be my only consideration. I wanted to live in Harlem to be among people like me, perhaps. But is skin color enough to indeed keep me safe and make me like them, to allow me to be accepted?

A cloud of confusion swirled about me there on the corner of 135th Street and Seventh Avenue. Suddenly I knew I didn't belong here. Suddenly I wasn't even sure I wanted to be in Harlem, why I had come, nor who I was.

Perhaps that is what I came to find out. Perhaps living this time here was my attempt to answer the who am I question.

Years ago I began to recognize my kinship with all living beings. . . . I said then as I say now, that while there is a lower class I am in it, while there is a criminal element, I am of it; while there is a soul in prison, I am not free.

—Eugene V. Debs, 1920

The streets of Harlem are paved no longer with gold. Instead the streets are filthy. The sidewalks are an obstacle course of garbage and dog shit. Mountains of trash sit piled up on just about every street and lure rats into the open to forage for food before they scurry back into the buildings they infest, buildings, many of them, that are very old and in need of repair. Even the newer ones seem somewhat decrepit.

Practically every street reeks of ruin, poverty, and despair, and you cannot move without the sense of danger forever present around you. The danger itself may come and go, may not even be real, but the sense of it never vanishes. As in the minds of the white folks too scared to venture this far uptown, Harlem might very well be the darkest, dirtiest, and most dangerous place on the face of this earth. If Harlem was ever once a paradise, it is certainly no longer that same paradise, certainly not in reality, but not even in the imagination.

Oddly enough, however, the myth remains somehow and

somewhat intact. Mysteriously *Harlem*, both the word and the place, still resonates with magic in the ears of many.

There is a woman, Olivia Maxwell, who even now sits in her kitchen in a Chicago public housing apartment and romanticizes about a Harlem that once was, envisioning a place she never knew, a place that was long ago. Its mission, its raison d'être, was in part to give concrete hope to people like Olivia who live lives of nothing but hope—and dreams unfulfilled.

She is a very large woman taking care of two small grandchildren. Her daughter, their mother, is a cocaine addict who professes for the ninety-ninth time that she is trying to kick the habit—for real, this time, she says. In the meantime, Olivia takes care of the children in a small apartment where we once sat in the kitchen and drank tea.

It was wintertime, fiercely cold outside. The wind that lashed in from Lake Michigan was biting enough to tear your flesh, wicked enough to rattle the windows in Olivia's apartment and to sneak in through the cracks. With each new gust of wind came a whistling sound and a draft. The kitchen was by far the warmest room in the apartment. The door was kept closed, and all four gas burners on the stove were lighted for the heat they gave.

"I would offer you some cake to go with the tea," she said, but she never completed the thought. She didn't need to.

This was life in a Chicago tenement, cold and cakeless. The furniture in the living room was old and ugly and had the look of a secondhand store showroom. Even at half the price it would have been too expensive. The kitchen table was part of a cheap dinette set that ought not last much more than a season or two beyond this one, but that had probably been around for ten and would probably go for ten more. The chairs did not match.

In the cupboard were rows and rows of canned soups, canned stews, canned vegetables, bags of potato chips, boxes of presweetened cereal. You can look in the cupboards of poor people all over the country, and this is what you will find. And most of it paid for with food stamps.

A roach crawled up the wall. I wouldn't have been surprised to see a mouse. Or worse.

Although Olivia's apartment was kept clean, the building itself was foul. It was a twenty-story high-rise. There were two elevators. They were old and slow. You could easily wait ten, maybe fifteen minutes for an elevator to come—if they both happened to be working. By then a small crowd would have gathered, and the elevator would be packed.

Better crowded than empty, for there was a decidedly dangerous feel to the place, especially to the elevator. Not only was it old and slow and run-down, and you felt all the while that it was about to break down, you also got the feeling that something else was about to happen. I don't know what. I don't know why. But there was the same sense of imminent danger that you feel often on the streets of Harlem. The lobby was crowded with many people just hanging around, many people coming and going, and there was a security guard stationed at a desk by the front door. He somehow added to the presence of danger when he should have alleviated it.

This is but one picture of black life, but an all too common one, and perhaps the picture that sticks most in the mind and becomes too often the representation of the whole of black life. It was definitely this image that Harlem as the new Jerusalem was supposed to alter or erase.

It was what the idea of Harlem once promised, and although I knew Harlem would not be as it had once been, in some vague way I was hoping for it—not necessarily the old image of Harlem as paradise, but the old feeling of Harlem as refuge. I felt the same going there, I think, as Olivia Maxwell might have felt.

When we spoke of Harlem, Olivia's eyes brightened for the first time.

"Why?" I asked her. "What is it about that place?"

"I have no idea," she said. "But I have always wanted to go there. If I ever get the chance to travel and if I could ever get to New York, the first thing I want to do is go to Harlem. 'Mister,' I would say to that taxi man. 'Take me up to Harlem.'"

"To do what?"

"Just be there," she said.

She admitted she knew nothing about Harlem but what she had seen in the movies and on TV, and what she had read and had been told. She knew it was rumored to be a very dangerous place, a poor place, but none of this mattered. It was a black place, a magic place, a place full of wonderful history.

"Just once before I die," she said, "I would like to go there and see it."

Such is the enduring myth of Harlem.

Something all our own. Something magical, full of wild possibilities, full of promise. Harlem. There has been nothing like it anywhere since.

This, I guess, was why I came. But in the widening light of dawn, things take new shape. Feelings change.

I have a vague sense suddenly of how I feel now when I walk these streets. I cannot yet articulate it, but it is a feeling that sneaks up on me each time I leave my apartment and stroll the neighborhood. If I tried right now to put it into words, the explanation would be lost in meaningless hysteria and hyperbole. I think I'll wait, for to answer is to call into question my being here at all.

Down the street from where I live, a car has been destroyed. The windows were shattered, the seats and the dashboard ripped out and tossed into the avenue, the car set on fire. Nothing remains but the burned-out shell.

You look at this burned-out car, you think you are looking at a crime. What you are seeing is only the result of the crime.

Three minutes' walk away, down to the corner of 127th Street and St. Nicholas Avenue, you can see the back side of a former apartment building that either reminds you of the car you just saw or makes you think of a war zone. The windows have all been blown out or boarded up. The entire face of the building is streaked with the scars of a fire. It is but the shell of a building, in front of which lies a fenced-in vacant lot covered with rocks and weeds, strewn with trash.

This, they tell me, is the nicer part of Harlem.

A few minutes from there, a walk down Manhattan Avenue leads you to row upon row of apartments where people live in units right beside units that have been gutted and boarded up. Young men stand on the front stoop steps and smoke dope. Down the street on another corner, money changes hands. Quite out in the open, drugs are sold in a flash of money unfolded, passed from one to another, a vial of cocaine slipped into a pocket. As you pass, your eyes meet the eyes of a man rocking on his heels in front of a building where people live—bad enough, but where children live too, and play. He mutters something. You think it's a greeting. You nod hello. Then his mumbling registers.

"Get you some, man, get you some right here."

Drugs for sale.

In a second-floor window a little child sits and watches it all as if she is watching a television. A young woman approaches, looks up, and shouts.

"Get out that window."

But she is only playing with the little girl, not concerned for the child's safety—not enough for my liking.

"Get out that window and go get your mama," the woman shouts.

The child still doesn't move. The woman screams up again in a voice big enough to rise above the noise on the street.

"Hey. Somebody up there throw me down a drill. I need me a drill."

To the window where the child still sits someone finally

comes and gets ready to throw hand tools down to the street. There seems little worry about the child sitting in an open window two floors above the ground, little concern from the apartment where the child lives, just as little from the street below. The child is just pushed aside.

Street after street, more and more of the same. All you see are the weeds winning over the neighborhood. You never stop to wonder how the weeds came to be planted or how long ago the seeds were sown. You only shake your head in disgust. You see what you think is a shame, but what you see really is the result of the shame.

I ask myself as I walk east across 111th Street: Is this what I came here for? I could be in the south of France, I said. I could be hiking the north Yorkshire moors. I could be living in Paris, for God's sake.

In fact, the season before I came to live in Harlem, I *had* spent in Paris, in London, and in Yorkshire. The season before that one I had spent in a seventeenth-century house almost as old as Harlem itself, and about as far removed from here as you can possibly get. It was in a little village called Montpeyroux in the southwest corner of France, the kind of place where you don't have to lock the front door. In fact I never locked up when I was away from the house. The only time I locked the door was when I was home and didn't want the neighbors, who when they dropped in for a visit would often enter without knocking.

I think back to my time in Montpeyroux; lazy days and even lazier nights, the biggest danger coming from the possibility of getting run over by a teenager on a moped. Quite possibly that is how life is supposed to be, safe and quiet and calm. Just as possibly, for me it was too calm. Perhaps I need a certain tension.

I had all the world to choose from. In fact I had chosen much of it, had traveled extensively and really seen the world, had lived in some of the world's greatest cities and felt at home in far-flung places and situations, had enjoyed bits and pieces of what many might consider *"the good life"*; why, then, would I want to live in Harlem? Why would I voluntarily choose to limit myself, I who had up to now done everything I could to extend my reach and broaden my horizons?

When you're black and American and aware of much that blacks ought to be aware of, for the sake of the others perhaps you cannot afford that kind of luxury for too long, the luxury of tranquillity. It is too easy to let your guard down. Too much comfort, too much easy living, can cause you to forget your pain, most certainly the pain of others. Too much comfort, and you might soon believe there is no pain.

I came to Harlem, it can be said, to put in my tour of duty on the front lines. To do what with the experience, I don't know. But at least to have it.

I had found the Harlem apartment where I wanted to live. It had been no easy task. Landlords and leasing agents would make appointments with me and then not show up. Or else they would show me apartments that were absolutely unsuitable for living in: filthy apartments, many of them, trash in the hallways, roaches living in bathroom sinks, wires exposed and hanging from holes in the ceiling. And this is not the condition of Harlem apartments scheduled for repair after years and years of use and misuse; these are very often the Harlem apartments they expect you to move into.

The landlords, most of them, don't live in Harlem, of course. They aren't going to be your neighbors. They don't care about you. They don't care how or where you live. They don't care about the apartments. Why should they? If *you* don't rent this place, someone else will—someone a bit more desperate perhaps than you, but someone, someone who will pay just as much as you.

Not much has changed in Harlem since its creation as a black ghetto. Then—as now, as probably always throughout

Harlem's history as a black community—rents have been higher here than in most other parts of the city for apartments of the same size. Even if what you spend is less than what you might spend for an apartment elsewhere in the city, you end up with very little for your money—or anyway less than what you might have if you lived farther downtown, all things considered. Often what you get in Harlem is not worth any amount of money.

I was once shown an apartment that rented for less than half what I ended up paying for the apartment I ultimately settled on. But no matter how much less, it wasn't enough less. It was in a decaying building on a decaying street not very far from the street where I finally came to live, but not nearly as nice. Its carpet was mildewed and smelled like rot, the walls were dingy, paint peeled from the ceiling, the apartment had no windows. It was a small one-room affair with a tiny bathroom off to one side. There was no kitchen. A small stove and a rusting refrigerator had been set up in the main room, but placed right behind the front door in a space so small you had to be careful when you entered. There was nothing else in the room but a back door that opened onto a rear courtyard—or it would have opened onto the courtyard if the back door had actually opened. The door was made of steel and had been welded shut for security.

The apartment could easily have passed for a prison cell, the building for some kind of halfway house. The main outside door was also made of steel, dented and bent on its hinges and difficult to open. It was scarred with a thousand names and initials carved with something sharp through the paint and into the metal.

Some of the people who lived in this building were sitting on the front stoop on the evening I came to look at the apartment. They had nothing better to do but fan themselves in the heat, sit on the steps, and smoke. A man who did not live there, I don't suppose, was banging on the heavy metal door and trying to get in. No one on the steps did or said anything to help him or to discourage him. The man showing me the apartment said nothing to him either. He, the landlord, just opened the door with his key, and we went inside. He didn't seem to care that the man banging on the door had followed us in.

But, as expected, the landlord didn't live in that building, didn't live in the neighborhood, didn't live anywhere near here. Why should he care what goes on in his building as long as he gets his rent—and gets it on time? He made it very clear that he disapproved of rent checks arriving late. He said he didn't like to have to come way uptown to hassle people about money. He lived, of course, somewhere downtown. He wouldn't tell me where.

Similarly, the man who owned the building where I eventually came to live did not live in the neighborhood either. He too, I presume, lives somewhere downtown, or out on Long Island, or in the upstate suburbs of New York. He doesn't live in Harlem, though. This I know, and I doubt if he comes up here very often.

He is a downtown lawyer, and his name is Levine. I know nothing else about him. I dealt only with his agent, a management company with offices on the Upper East Side. I went there only once, although I have often wondered if theirs is one of the buildings I can see from the window of my apartment as I look into the distance, to that other world down and across Central Park.

My normal dealings with them came only once a month when I sent them the rent check. Although I know firsthand that they don't easily tolerate late rent checks either.

TAKE NOTICE: THAT YOU ARE JUSTLY INDEBTED TO THE LANDLORD OF THE ABOVE PREMISES IN THE SUM OF $750.00 FOR RENT OF SAID PREMISES WHICH YOU ARE HEREBY REQUESTED TO PAY ON OR BEFORE THE EXPIRATION OF THREE DAYS FROM RECEIPT OF THIS NOTICE, IN DEFAULT OF WHICH THE LANDLORD WILL EXERCISE HIS LEGAL REMEDY, THE COST OF WHICH MAY BE ADDED TO YOUR BALANCE DUE.

Halfway through my first year in Harlem I received this notice in my mailbox. I had been out of town and had sent the rent from wherever I was. Either it took longer to reach the office than I thought it would take, or else the check was received but not recorded because I hadn't included the computerized invoice I was supposed to send along with my payment. Regardless, the check couldn't have been more than a day or two late. But here came the notice and threats of legal action.

I in reply wrote a biting letter of my own, pointing out that this was no way to deal with a tenant, since the rent had not been late before, and I wondered why they should panic so quickly now. If they were going to be so worried about my ability to pay—justly, as it later turned out—perhaps they shouldn't have rented the apartment to me in the first place. I also wondered why they would jump straightaway into threats of legal action instead of sending a letter of inquiry, a gentle reminder perhaps that I was delinquent, or why not wait a few days to see just how late the check would arrive?—if indeed it would arrive.

By the time I got the notice, my check had appeared. And they had already cashed it. I told them that I naturally expected an apology, knew of course that I would not get one, and so told them into which of a series of lakes they could all go and jump. I told them as well just where they could shove their notices, their writs, and all manner of threats they cared to send. I also said in the letter that I wished them a nice day.

I heard nothing back from them. Nor was I pestered ever again when I was late with the rent. And I did not feel particularly guilty when my money finally ran out and it was a struggle to pay the rent at all, whether on time or late.

I did not work for pay while I lived in Harlem. As much as possible I wanted to live the life I saw around me, wanted to be one of the men I saw with nothing to do, nowhere to go. I wanted to live the black experience that has become the cliché, the black experience that I had come to believe. I don't know why I believed it. It was far from any black experience I had ever known—at least up close—but I had come somehow to believe it, and I wanted to live it. So I allowed myself to become poor, desperate for money, and without the means of easily getting my hands on more—not anytime soon, anyway.

In my diary I find this entry:

I have lived in Harlem so far now for almost one full year. . . . Mice and roaches are conspiring to take over my kitchen and nothing I do seems to help. They can't be after food; there is nothing here to eat. There is nothing in the refrigerator, only staples on the cupboard shelves: rice, beans, flour for biscuits, cereal for breakfast, a chicken frozen in the freezer. Winter this year promises to be especially long and severe. As its approaching shadow lengthens and expands, my money supply continues to shrink. I have $1,293 in the bank; no immediate prospects for more. $1,293 is not much money in New York City. The rent is more than half of what I have and due in eight days. And there are other bills to pay. Do I pay the bills or do I pay the rent? Or should I buy groceries? I know I am not, but these days I feel very very poor.

—November 22

I was really living the life now, I thought.

What I didn't think, and what I now know to be true, was that I was slipping deeper and deeper into the trap.

As money became more of a problem, I became less and less prompt with the rent payments, but by then I cared nothing about the landlords and their cash flow, no more than they cared about me and mine—apart, that is, from my ability to pay the rent.

Send it, and send it damn quick: Pig Foot Mary all over again.

Harlem is as Harlem was. There is little difference between Pig Foot Mary and Mr. Levine; there never has been. Harlem is not and has never been paradise—not with white landlords, not with black landlords. Harlem is still Harlem, a hard place to be.

One night, in the middle of the night, my father asked what would seem for him a very unlikely question. He wanted to know why I wanted to live in Harlem.

It was about three o'clock in the morning. We had been up all day and all night. Now we were racing to get back home and speeding toward St. Louis. We had been out traveling again; I was once more and forever the sidekick.

I have never seen my father so thoughtful as he was that night, as if, like an old man in a melodrama, he was anticipating some disaster or expecting to die.

After I had found the right apartment in the right part of Harlem, while the building managers had the place cleaned and did whatever they do that prevents you from moving in straightaway, I had gone home to St. Louis. When I went back to New York to sign the lease, to hand over money, and to collect the keys, my father had come with me. He had wanted to look over the apartment, see what I was up to, and make sure everything was all right. He still worries about me. I guess I will always be his little boy, just as I will forever be the sidekick.

To find this apartment I had tried adverts in the newspapers, I had tried calling the numbers on the For Rent signs I had seen when I walked the neighborhoods, I had tried asking strangers on the street. Finding an apartment in New York City is tough enough; finding one in Harlem seemed quite impossible. But I knew somebody who knew somebody who used to live in Harlem, and she had used a Harlem agency to help her find an apartment. I got the name of that agency, and they helped me too.

There is, of course, a hefty fee attached to using a rental agency: an amount equal to one month's rent. Along with the agency fee you need an additional month's rent for a security deposit, as well as the first month's rent itself. You need, in short, a fairly good chunk of money to get a place to live in Harlem, and you need it every time you want to move. If you've not got a lot of money, you always start off in a hole. If you've not got a lot of money, you can easily find yourself stuck in a place because you can't afford to move.

I have the answer now when people ask—and people do ask me—why, considering the reputed plight of the place, Harlemites don't just move away. I tell them that moving away is sometimes harder than it seems.

My father and I left the offices of the management company on Third Avenue. I had signed the lease, had taken the keys, had surrendered the rent and the security deposit. But we still had to go back to Harlem to the rental agency and pay them their fee. My father decided not to come along. He wanted to walk the neighborhood a bit. So I dropped him off on the corner of 145th and St. Nicholas and told him I would be back for him in forty minutes.

When I returned, my father was standing in front of a

liquor store midway up the block. He was wearing baggy brown trousers. The cuffs dragged on the ground. A half pint of cheap bourbon was stuck in his back pocket. From time to time he would take a little swig from it. The rest of the time he stood there with his hands behind his back, stood there observing everything, just stood there trying to be as inconspicuous as possible.

He wore a baseball cap that day with the bill turned around not quite backward as the current style dictated, but rather sideways. Instead of looking like a tough guy hanging on the streets, he looked almost demented, the more so because he just stood there, rocking on the balls of his feet, his hands behind his back, doing nothing else.

Movement is what makes New York City. To stand still in the middle of the block for more than a few minutes is not often done here. Apart from shifting his weight, my father's only movement was to now and again take the bottle from his pocket and have another sip. He was about as inconspicuous as an icicle in July. He did not look like he belonged here.

He told me later that he wanted to look a little crazy so nobody would bother him. He had gotten his wish. People passing stepped well away from him before going by, probably half expecting him to ask for a handout. He had not shaved that morning, his shirt was not tucked in very neatly, and all of the buttons were not done up. His big belly pushed through the opening. He might very easily have awakened recently from a night in a doorway and now was drinking away his hangover, begging loose change for his breakfast.

That is the image he offered this day to the world around him. To me, watching him from across the street, he looked at first very comical, and as I laughed at him I wondered if this could possibly have been the same man who had given me my sense of sartorial style. He had always kept himself so neat, was always so well-dressed. There was a flair about him, an élan that I attributed to all black men, for the black men of my youth—or at least in my memory—always wanted to look good. They would not dream of ever leaving the house, except maybe when laboring manually, unless they thought they were sharply dressed.

Those days are long gone now. My father is a little out of practice. He lives most of his life these days lounging around the house in a bathrobe.

I watched him for a few minutes and remembered the old man when he was young, all pride and dignity. Now he seemed a little silly, easily disregarded. I laughed for a few minutes at him and at the way people looked at him until suddenly I stopped. Seeing him like this and knowing how he used to be, the sight of him wasn't funny anymore.

All at once I was wondering if this was the same man who had branded me when I was young with the fierce pride I carry, the same man who helped to give me my sense of myself. Where was the pride in his appearance, where was his self-awareness? I was almost angry with him for not caring how he looks anymore, for having given up, for having let his youth and his pride and somehow even his hope all slip away.

The anger turned to sorrow when I saw how old and how

tired he seemed. I know much of what he has been through. I have heard all the stories. And I could see by the look in his eyes that here was a man a little bit lost. He was in his world again, that's true, but this was not the world he ever knew. This was not the world he had ever hoped for.

My father comes from a time and from a place where almost everything he did was for his children and for his family. You could say he lived the life he lived for the sake of the future, that he and other men like him did what they did for the ones who would follow. The Harlem my father saw that day was probably not what he—not what *they*—had in mind.

If they had thought consciously at all about these things, my father and the men and women who were like him, they might have thought they were making a garden, might have thought they were tilling rich soil and making it fertile. They would not have considered, and perhaps they should have, that they were planting along with the roses the roots of a weed bed.

For a time Harlem was the kind of garden that is magical: something made out of nothing, for nothing was what they had to work with, nothing but their souls and their hopes, a spirit and a dream. And with not much more than these was made something glorious, something fruitful, and much more important, something made with their own hands, their own efforts. Something to be proud of. Something all their own. Something finally in their own image and likeness.

If, that is, they had their own image, their own likeness, and were not merely reflecting someone else's image, someone else's likeness, nor someone else's image of who they were, who and how they ought to remain.

They came to create in the garden something that had not been before—something *they* had not been before, something they had not been allowed to be, but something, after such a long time in the darkness, hands, feet, and spirits bound, something they wanted to try. They were creating a new way to be who they were, a way to be who they yearned to be. Finally now they were free to choose. Harlem was where they chose to do it.

Not that there hadn't been then and have not since been other significant black communities. In fact even as Harlem was being planted and was taking shape, every city north and south—same as now—had its Nigger Alley, its Coontown, its dark side of the tracks where the black folks lived. And as Harlem was a long time in the making, these other communities too were the same long time in the making, created perforce out of the same conditions that had created Harlem then and that have made Harlem what it has become today: the same seeds planted deep in similar soil, comparably nurtured, and fertilized with the same never-ending supply of manure.

These black towns and black sections of other towns and cities tried to achieve something on the order of Harlem, but somehow Harlem was always different. Somehow Harlem became the center of the black universe.

Perhaps for no other reason than that it was New York City, already the center of a certain universe. Conditions there were perfect for an explosion. The time was certainly right.

The world in general had caused it; the world in general was ready for it. It could even be said that the world was in need of it. The black world in particular needed it too and was definitely ripe for it, ripe enough to burst forth with succulent juices all its own, ripe enough and ready set to split open like a busted watermelon and then to spill far and wide the seeds of its pent-up passions, appetites and emotions. Harlem.

Suddenly the earth tilted on its axis an extra three degrees, and the moon and the stars aligned just so. The tide swelled and the ocean roared, and when the wind blew, the word was whispered across the land and across the seas. Harlem.

Harlem!

Harlem did not spring forth in full bloom, of course. Its seeds long ago had been planted in the soil of a national constitution that recognized black men as only three-fifths of a whole man and didn't recognize black women at all, and that gave neither black men nor women any rights of citizenship. Its roots lay gently cradled in the soft loam of extreme prejudice. They were fertilized daily within a nation's Christian conscience and watered with care, the tender shoots covered over and kept warm with an abundance of dung.

It was a long time, indeed, to the making of Harlem, a long time from tending the soil to first planting, a long time from the garden until the weeds took over. You have only to live here to see what too much care—the wrong kind of care and the wrong kind of fertilizer—can do to poison the soil. You have only to visit here to see the making of Harlem made complete, perhaps now in fullest flower, the final effects of too much neglect. The weeds have won.

It is a very long way from the Harlem of hope to the Harlem of despair, from the flower garden to the weeds, but once there grew here the kind of magic that even time and distance could not easily dim, the kind of magic that gives concrete hope to the lives of people like Olivia Maxwell in Chicago, the hope that out there somewhere black people are living lives that are glamorous and beautiful and really worth living.

Forty, fifty, seventy-five years ago, when Harlem was still Harlem, still the Blackamerican mecca, and indeed a mecca for black people the world over, when Harlem as the Harlem we know was still young and new and magical, this place had the power within its self-created myth to make black people feel free just by being here.

It is a long road from where we've been to where we are now, from where we've been and where we are to where we are *not* now, a long way from the days of old when Harlem—as they say—was really Harlem, days long ago when jazz was king and Edward Kennedy Ellington was the Duke, a time when the A train, instead of being dreaded, was part of Harlem's amazing enchantment.

The music plays in my head each and every time I enter the subway and board that train, Billy Strayhorn's music, Duke Ellington's band, the satin voice of Ella Fitzgerald, and I call to mind what once was, a world long past.

You must take the A train to go to Sugar Hill way up in Harlem. If you miss the A train, you'll find you've missed the quickest way to Harlem.

As he stood in dismay waiting for me on 145th Street that afternoon, my father too must have been reminded of how it used to be when the world was full of change and hope and possibility, when, as I offered to those ladies selling barbecue on that street corner in St. Louis, being black was a whole lot of fun.

I could see my father wondering where it had all gone.

Harlem before it burned itself out must have been *really something else*. Anyone who knows anything about the Harlem of those days will tell you so. It was more than a mere place. It was a spirit, a zeitgeist, more than just some neighborhood, the same as it is more than just some neighborhood now. Then as now, for so many black people throughout the world Harlem meant something truly special—and not the same something special that it means today. Harlem then, even with its problems, was full of hope. If you were young and if you were black, if you wanted change, a taste of freedom perhaps or a little excitement, then Harlem was where you longed to be.

Harlem was the Promised Land, where black men and women came to escape, came to reach beyond the grasp they would have been able to reach for in the places they came from, came at the very least to dream the dreams that might have gone unimagined. They came to make real the impossible. For those coming up from the Deep South, Harlem was the last stop on the long journey now called the Great Migration, when the steady stream of blacks that had been flowing out of the South since the end of the Civil War became like a torrent.

Out of the South they fled, as far away as possible from the lynchman's noose and the Jim Crow laws designed to keep a black man from being treated like a man, far away from the culture that saw nothing wrong with black men being lynched as if for sport, doused with gasoline and set on fire, driven from their homes and shot like hogs. In the South, it seemed, no act of terror was indefensible in the noble effort to keep blacks in their ordained and proper place of complete misery: ignorant and lowly, without hope or opportunity. Racism suddenly had taken a turn for the worse, if such a thing were possible, and white supremacy descended to new depths of viciousness, virulence, and angry violence. The first wave of the Great Migration was more like the flight out of Egypt.

"Every time a lynching takes place in a community down South," said T. Arnold Hill, head of the Chicago Urban League, "you can depend on it that colored people will arrive in Chicago within two weeks."

He could as easily have been referring to New York City, or to Detroit, or to any other city in the North. Not that the Mason-Dixon line was any kind of barrier to intense racial hatreds. Up North as well as down South, lynchings still took place. Up North as well as down South, there was mob violence against blacks. Up North as well as down South, the demons discrimination and color prejudice were woven so tightly into the fabric of American life and American thinking that there had never yet been a time—perhaps still has not yet been a time—in American history when blacks could feel the full weight of their right to liberty, to life, and to the pursuit of happiness. They had never been then, perhaps have never been yet, fully accepted, North or South, as American citizens—nor even, it could be said, as human beings.

To say that life was unfair for Blackamericans would be to state the ridiculously obvious.

In the middle of the nineteenth century Irish and German immigrants were learning to flex political muscle as a means toward their advancement. Most native-born blacks were not even allowed to vote—not in the South, not in the North.

In New York City, where the foundations for Harlem as a black community were being laid, even after blacks had been given the right to vote they still had to meet residency requirements stricter than the requirements for whites. Long after property ownership requirements had been removed for all other New Yorkers, blacks still had to meet them. Out of a population of ten thousand blacks in 1865, only forty-four were eligible to vote.

Blacks in New York City were denied equal access to almost all public facilities, including public education. In white Christian churches they were forced to sit in designated sections. All over Manhattan, right until the end of the Civil War, there were the signs: For Colored People Only.

Harlem, of course, had to happen. Whites had made it clear that they cared little about the concerns of blacks.

Even after the great New York City race riot of 1900, whites still refused to pay serious attention to black demands for justice and equality. In fact, when the rioting had ended, it was reported that many whites in New York admitted they would have been happier if the blacks who had been merely injured had instead been killed. Newspapers reported that the angry mobs of whites attacking blacks could easily have been broken up but that the police did nothing to offer protection. The police actually abetted the rioters, taking defenseless men and women and throwing them to the angry crowds. In many cases the police beat blacks more savagely than the rioters themselves.

The riot was sparked when Arthur Harris saw his wife in the grasp of a plainclothes police officer and ran to her defense. The policeman clubbed him, knocked him down, and shouted, "Get up, you black son of a bitch." Trying to protect himself, he said, and not knowing the man was a police officer, Harris fought back and stabbed him. The policeman died two days later. The following day the dead cop's neighborhood erupted in retaliation.

Blacks were chased, attacked, dragged from buses and streetcars, and beaten. Any black person who happened to be on the street that day and night was assaulted.

William Elliott was arrested for carrying a pistol. He was taken apparently unharmed to the Thirty-seventh Street police station. By the time he left, his brains had been beaten out of his head.

Area hospitals were full of black people whose heads had been bashed in. The local police courts were jammed with black people who had been arrested. When an outraged magistrate demanded that some of the white rioters be brought before him as well, one lone teenager was hauled in. He was accused of trying to trip a police officer.

Yet in the aftermath of these riots, the *New York Times* went so far as to make the curious claim that there were no signs that blacks were distrusted or disliked, stating, in fact, the contrary: *"His crude melodies and childlike antics are more than tolerated. . . ."*

Henry Turner, a bishop in Georgia, said plainly, *"Hell would be an improvement upon the United States when the Negro is involved."*

"No man hates this Nation more than I do," he said.

Harlem had to happen, a place where blacks could be apart and away from this kind of injustice. They needed a place of their own, a place where they could feel they belonged, a place where they could be part of something, a place where impossible dreams could anyway be dreamed.

Blacks by and large had missed out on land allotted under the Homestead Act. This, then, would have to be their collective plot. Harlem as no other place would be theirs.

Blackamerica needed Harlem. Oddly enough, Harlem needed Blackamerica. The time was right for it.

If it had been a question only of fleeing the reign of terror, degradation, and racial violence that rampaged in the South, black men and women would have fled long before they did. They would have escaped as soon after the destruction of slavery as they had been able. If it had been a question of economics only and the search for jobs, the Great Migration would have been greatest during the industrial boom of the 1870s.

But rather, some unseen hand was at work here, some strange force far subtler and more insidious even than merely time and circumstance, something far more akin to the influence of stars and planets, perhaps, than to that which can be plotted on social and economic flow charts.

Out of the South they came, these black men and women, out of the South and ready for something new, a new generation ready to *be* something new.

By then of course blacks had been living in Manhattan for close to three hundred years, since 1626 when it was still a Dutch settlement called New Amsterdam and eleven Africans were imported to work as indentured servants. After 1664 other blacks began to arrive. The Dutch had given way by then to the English. New Amsterdam had become New York. The indentured servants had become slaves.

Some of the blacks lived even then in the village called Harlem, but by the time slavery was abolished in New York in 1827, most blacks lived on the south end of the island. By the time of the 1830 census there were 13,976 blacks living in New York. Most of them had been born there.

By the end of the century, however, more than half the black population had been born elsewhere.

Certainly they came from other parts of the United States, from the islands in the Caribbean, from all around the black universe, but by and large the new arrivals to New York City came from the Deep South, bringing with them their music, their food, their language and religion, influencing and perhaps even laying the foundation for an entire culture.

Out of the South they came: the businessmen, the educated, the politicians, and the skilled workers; but came too the unskilled workers, the cooks and the maids, the waiters, the coachmen, the physical laborers; came too even those who had fewer skills than these, many of them vagrants, vagabonds, and criminals, some out for a taste of city life, some who came only to see and then never went back, some running away from home. Some wanted nothing more than a change. All of them were part of the new generation of blacks with whom the elements of nature and time had conspired. For these who came were not merely answering the call to the big city. These who came were responding to circumstances created in part by the end of slavery. These who came were not the former slaves themselves but the sons of slaves, the daughters of slaves, the grandchildren of slaves. They were a new kind of Blackamerican evolving out of the old. They had not experienced in the same way as their parents and grandparents so complete and abject a denial of their humanity. They wanted to expand and grow. They thought they owned a piece of the future.

For the most part the older generation continued even in freedom the lives they had known in slavery days. As sharecroppers and tenant farmers now, they worked the same land they had once worked as slaves. They could conceive of little else.

The new generation, however, wanted more. Surely they came to escape the South's restrictions on what they could and could not do, who they could and could not be, and surely they were fleeing the violence of the South and a culture that reserved for them only the chaff and the dregs, at best. Just as surely they came to earn the higher wages offered in the mechanized North. But what their parents and grandparents could hardly fathom, what the whites who needed their labors on farms throughout the South refused to recognize, was what really drew the new generation, the New Negro, as he called himself, to places like New York City, and specifically to this place called Harlem. It was to create a new identity.

The world around them was in the midst of enormous social evolution. In the North institutionalized racism was under siege. Laws were being passed attempting to guarantee equal rights for blacks. Since 1873 they could vote in New York State without impediment. Because of new legislation they could now, at least by law, share buses and trains with whites, go to the same theaters, eat in the same restaurants, be buried in the same public cemeteries.

In the 1880s a black man served on a New York City jury. Separate education ended when the last three black schools were brought into the same system as other public schools. Ten years later Susan Frazier became the first black teacher in a white public school.

It wasn't utopia; there was still discrimination, still a lot of racial hatred; but the world was in transition. Now there was possibility.

Now too came the explosion, and the numbers more than doubled. In the final decade of the nineteenth century over a hundred thousand blacks fled the South, twenty-five thousand to New York City alone. Between 1890 and 1910 two hundred thousand additional blacks had migrated to cities in the North and the West.

In *Harlem: The Making of a Ghetto*, Gilbert Osofsky writes, "The most important factor underlying the establishment of Harlem as a Negro community was the substantial increase of Negro population in New York City in the years 1890–1914."

The black population of New York City had tripled.

It was all boiling together now. The moon and the stars and all the planets were on the move. The industrialization of the late nineteenth century was gathering steam and needed manpower. The Great Migration was on full blast. Harlem as *Harlem* was becoming inevitable.

Came then the world war, and with it more black immigrants. The war machine, like the industrial machine, needed manpower. Blacks fled the farm and aimed for the city to power the machinery that European immigration had previously helped to fuel, but which now because of the war had fallen off. When the war ended, blacks were still coming, from the South certainly, but from the Caribbean as well, assisted by the immigration laws of the 1920s, which had severely curtailed the influx of Europeans but virtually ignored islanders from the West Indies.

And so they came. Oh! how they came, these blacks from the South and from the islands, came to make Harlem, came seeking the future, but came as well to escape, for with the increasing numbers of blacks came the typical knee-jerk reaction of whites sensing that the invader has simply gone too far, either in number or in overstepping the bounds of freedoms, rights and equalities that black people ought to be allowed: racial discord, separation and further alienation.

White churches that had once received blacks, as long as they were small in number and sat in separate pews, now told them they were not welcome at all, now told them to get churches of their own.

The same was happening in white hotels, restaurants, and theaters. Blacks were no longer able to get service. A separate YMCA was built to keep black people out of the facilities that white folks used.

In a climate of rampant anxiety at the increasing black population, efforts were advanced to roll back measures that had been intended to ease racial tensions and prejudice. There was even a proposal to void all marriages that had taken place between *"a person of the white or Caucasian race and a person of the negro or black race."*

Blacks were kept out of the unions and out of all but the most menial and worst-paying jobs: janitors and street sweepers, porters, elevator operators, waiters, and shoe shiners. Blacks were kept on the fringe, largely unemployed, certainly underemployed, not worthy of great concern.

Black people needed refuge from a world that, according to the *New York Freeman,* saw them "more as a problem than as a factor in the general weal, with the same desires, passions, hopes, ambitions as other human creatures."

These are the conditions and climate that created the despair that created the hope that created Harlem, the city of refuge, the city that became the black mecca.

In March 1925, the *Survey Graphic* ran a special issue

called *Harlem: Mecca of the New Negro*, where, in an essay simply titled "Harlem," Alain Locke wrote, *"Harlem had the same role to play for the New Negro as Dublin has had for the New Ireland or Prague for the New Czechoslovakia."*

Adam Clayton Powell Sr. called Harlem *"the symbol of liberty and the Promised Land to Negroes everywhere."*

Eslanda Robeson said that only blacks belonged in Harlem. "It is," she said, "a place they can call home."

And home was what they needed.

So they moved to the suburbs.

Harlem, as a matter of fact, used to be the suburbs.

That is probably hard to believe, standing where we now stand and seeing the urban decay all around.

Standing where my father stood, I would have found it hard to imagine, had I tried, that Harlem had ever been anything but what it was that day, and certainly not a pastoral community of prosperous farmers, colonial families, peace and tranquillity. Marshes and meadows covered the district of Harlem then, clean streams, goats and geese and cows. Eventually, though, the land played out. The farms were abandoned, many of the great estates were sold at public auction, property values plunged.

As longtime residents moved out, Irish immigrants moved in. They built shanties and shacks and squatted on abandoned lands that had formerly been prosperous estates. Those who could buy property did so cheaply. They built small houses. Harlem was fast becoming a residential community. And new prosperity was on its way.

Harlem was still the country, a rural outing for city dwellers, a weekend in the countryside where downtowners could get away from New York and take afternoon strolls along the quiet lanes. The aristocratic horsey set would ride their sulkies through Central Park to exercise their trotters on Harlem Lane—long before it became St. Nicholas Avenue—and people wanting to avoid the frenzy of New York City began moving to Harlem to escape the noise and the crowds of the city and to get away from the next wave of immigrants who had newly arrived.

They couldn't escape for long.

Once the population of New York City had passed the one-million mark, pastoral Harlem's days were numbered. There was nowhere else for a city built on an island to grow, nowhere to put all those people except for them to move north.

Finally in 1873 Harlem was annexed to New York City. Three elevated train lines were extended into Harlem, and Harlem quickly became the scene of wild speculation and development. Nearly all the houses that exist still today in Harlem were built in the frenzy that followed.

Land changed hands often and quickly. Speculators made fortunes buying up Harlem real estate and selling it at tremendous profit to developers who built houses on the land and sold them quickly to reinvest the profit in still more buildings.

Prices soared. Rents in the new buildings were so high that only the wealthy could afford them. Harlem was poised to become an upper-class community.

Blacks of course still lived in the area. They had always lived in the area. They had been of course among the earliest settlers—if indeed slaves can be called settlers. They had tended the farms, worked the estates, and built the roads. The original wagon road connecting Harlem with the community farther down the island had in fact been built by black slaves. They even had their own burial ground.

With the end of slavery, blacks stayed in Harlem and began to spread across the area. They were squatters on abandoned lands long before the Irish immigrants were, or they farmed their own land, or they worked as servants in the mansions of the wealthy who were moving to Harlem. There was never a time when blacks did not live here.

But early in the twentieth century, when the second wave of real estate development collapsed, so many blacks suddenly began to appear in Harlem that white residents seemed to forget that substantial numbers of blacks had always lived here. These old white residents were shocked and dismayed and none too happy at the changes happening to their neighborhood.

Nowadays when we think of Harlem, we never think of it as *their* neighborhood. It is hard to remember that white folks once lived here too. It is hard to imagine a time when Harlem wasn't predominantly black—or even entirely black. It is so easy to look and see the world and think that everything is as everything always has been, possibly even that things will be forever as they are now.

When you stand on a street corner in Harlem you can easily get the feeling too that Harlem has always been this way and will always be this way, that Harlem has always been poor and desperate and dangerous, and that these things have always been equated somehow with being black.

It is easy to forget how disadvantage and atrophy happen, easy to forget how much we help them along.

The land speculation in Harlem continued unabated. Property values were inflated beyond the barriers of reality, yet new houses continued to be built. A new subway line had been proposed. It was supposed to make Harlem even more attractive, even more popular, justifying all the construction and the crazy high prices of rents and properties.

Then all at once the bubble burst. The subway that was proposed and then promised didn't arrive on time; and in anticipation of its arrival, too many buildings had been built. Harlem was awash in vacant apartments.

Now suddenly rents were too high, and landlords were forced into the dramatic action of lowering rents and allowing blacks to fill the vacancies. The boom was over. Blacks in large numbers began moving to Harlem.

Before Harlem turned into the fringe area it became, blacks in New York City had lived primarily in another fringe neighborhood, the Tenderloin—midtown Manhattan, along the West Side. Now with the construction of the new Pennsylvania Station came the destruction of many all-black tenement blocks. Displaced and now at last offered decent housing for the very first time, blacks moved in droves uptown to Harlem.

Landlords and speculators had been facing financial ruin, many of them. Some offered their apartments to blacks. Others used the threat of black tenants moving in to force whites in the neighborhood to buy the vacant properties. Still others allowed black tenants in order to further lower property values so they could buy buildings cheaply, often at half price, and then put in more black tenants once they discovered that blacks were willing to pay a premium to rent in Harlem.

Philip Payton found an opportunity here. New York's black population had been steadily growing and needed housing. And Payton knew how willing they would be to sacrifice and pinch pennies in order to live in such an exclusive area as Harlem. Payton, a black man, assured white landlords an income by leasing their apartment buildings. He then turned around and rented apartments to black tenants—at a 10 percent premium, of course.

Payton got control of his first building when two landlords were locked in a dispute. To get even with the other, one of the angry landlords turned his building over to Payton. Payton filled it with black families.

This was the beginning. Harlem was becoming a black community. Harlem would soon be the mecca it became. Harlem was turning first into a ghetto; then it turned into a slum. The slum is what we know of Harlem today.

We think we know this place because it is so much in our consciousness. We think we know Harlem because of the rumors we've heard, the movies we've seen, the stories we've read. We think we know this place because it is so deeply embedded in our cultural idiom that the very mention of Harlem conjures an image—perhaps not always the same image, but an image and a connotation. We think we are so familiar with this place that we know its history, its beginnings and endings, and the failings it has come to symbolize. We think of Harlem now, many of us, if we think of it at all, as we think perhaps of a dying fruit tree, or of a well gone dry. And we think we know—not that we care—but we think we know what happened.

There was a time—not so very long ago but still a long time ago, and perhaps we've forgotten—but there was a time after Harlem became the ghetto and while it was still the mecca when Harlem was a celebration.

It was a time so much like today and yet so unlike today. It was an era when white was white and black was black and Harlem meant nothing but blackness and the whites of this world did not want to live anywhere near the blacks of this world. It was this separate world of blackness that Harlem came to represent. It became a magnet for blacks the world over—certainly for blacks, but it became for a time a magnet for whites as well. It was dark—yes! forever dark, this place—but the darkness was of mystery, not so much of danger. Harlem was on the move, on the rise, full of life and hope. Harlem was fun.

It was, as Duke Ellington exclaimed when he first got here, like something out of the Arabian Nights, a time of amazing excitement, incredible frolic and carousing.

In *Parties*, Carl Van Vechten's novel of this early era, one character tells another: "And we'll get drunker and drunker and drift about night clubs so drunk that we won't know where we are, and then we'll go to Harlem and stay up all night and go to bed late tomorrow morning and wake up and begin it all over again."

Harlem was where you went to cap festive evenings—

and that was only if you hadn't started the partying there. 'Round about midnight the Harlem bands started swinging, the joints started jumping, and Harlem exploded with merriment.

You didn't want to live there if you were white, but you wanted to go there: to the Cotton Club, to Pod's and Jerry's Catagonia Club, to Tillie's Inn; to hear Duke Ellington's band, Fletcher Henderson's, Cab Calloway.

Harlem was a wondrous destination on a magical tour of nightclubs, music, and liquor, exotic living and excess. Harlem was full of life. Harlem was the place to be.

If uptown was, as Harlem on the surface might have seemed and as Van Vechten titled it in another novel, a kind of "Nigger Heaven" to blacks, it was for whites a different kind of paradise. When the Broadway shows let out and the dining was done, the white folks went uptown for a taste of the exotic, stayed until the wee hours, and then glided back downtown.

This is the Harlem of legend, the place we think we know. If we think of Harlem, this mythic Harlem is very often the Harlem we call to mind, that era of hot nights and swinging jazz and what is now called the renaissance of black art and literature, but was in fact the first birth of a black voice, the finding of a new black identity.

Nowadays another image of Harlem has taken the place of the previous one. Nowadays we look at Harlem and see nothing glamorous here. Exciting, perhaps—in a way. Dangerous, yes. Even exotic. But glamorous? There is nothing in the reports of Harlem, nothing in the modern definitions of Harlem, that suggests allure or appeal. The Arabian Nights have given way to the bitter reality of morning's harsh light, morning in America.

When the white folks had had enough of Harlem, they slid back downtown, out of sight, gone from here. They abandoned Harlem as if they were refugees fleeing a battle zone.

They stayed as long as they could. When the black invasion began, white owners organized into neighborhood associations to repulse the enemy. They advertised for white tenants, they pleaded with other whites to join the antiblack crusade, to protect themselves, protect their property, and keep their property values up by keeping blacks out. They devised covenants among themselves, promising not to rent and not to sell to blacks. It was even suggested (by John Taylor, founder of the Harlem Property Owners' Improvement Corporation) to white people living on the borders of black blocks that they build twenty-foot fences to separate themselves from their black neighbors.

They resisted the black hordes for as long as they could, but it was a lost cause. Too many white landlords were losing money. Real estate values spiraled downward. Buildings sold at bargain rates. Owners who had honored agreements not to sell or rent to blacks found no whites willing to rent. To keep the tenants they already had, they had to reduce rents still further. Many simply sold out. Many lost out to foreclosure. Many others stared at the dilemma: to stick to a policy trying to keep Harlem white and risk losing everything, or to rent to blacks—at higher prices, of course.

In the end the white folks gave up on Harlem. They

surrendered. They abandoned Harlem, abandoned their homes, abandoned property as if they were fleeing and seeking refuge elsewhere.

Harlem became black.

Then Harlem became mecca.

Said one black man: "If my race can make Harlem, good lord, what can't it do?"

It didn't happen overnight, but it happened. Harlem went from being a neighborhood where blacks could finally get decent housing to becoming the black part of town to becoming, as James Weldon Johnson put it, "the greatest Negro city in the world," a source of black pride, a place of enterprise for black people, a place of hope for black people.

Then Harlem became a slum.

I don't know what my father was thinking as he stood there and watched the street that day. I don't know how much of Harlem's history he knows. But whether we're talking about Harlem or about East St. Louis or about East Palo Alto or about the black parts of every town and every city in this country, the process of segregating blacks from whites has always been the same—the process and the end result—and he would have seen it all.

As a young man traveling, my father would have seen these Niggertowns and Black Bottoms, as they were called, the Smoketowns and the Bronzevilles. As a younger man growing up, he would have lived in them. As a young black man knowing nothing else, it might all have seemed so normal. I couldn't help but wonder, however, if he didn't feel a little bit cheated, a little bit angry. I certainly would have been. In fact I certainly was.

My own anger turned to sorrow then when I saw that sad look in his eyes as he watched all around him and saw the decay that had taken over from the garden that should have been.

Harlem held on to its original mission for a long time. It could not, it seems, hold out forever. The weeds finally own this garden, and I could see, again by the look in his eye, that my father himself was wondering where it had all gone, where it had all gone wrong. He was not only wondering what in the world had happened, he was questioning why it had happened.

He has the same watery eyes that I have, and when he fills with emotion it looks very often as if he is about to cry.

My anger turned to sorrow when I saw that look in his eye.

He said to me in the car that night as we made the long drive home, "Do you ever get the feeling that we're doing everything all wrong and that something just isn't right, that this is not the way things are supposed to be?"

"Pop," I said. "I get that feeling all the time."

I also had the feeling that he wasn't really talking to me.

*T*here is an old man with milky eyes who stands each warm day on the corner near his apartment building. His hands shake with a kind of palsy. His fingers are long and bony, his knuckles gnarled. Every now and again he takes a dingy white handkerchief from the pocket of his pants, the same brown trousers he wears every day, and he wipes the summer sweat from his brow. His hand, ever trembling, lingers near his eyes.

He might easily have been blotting away a tear, but it is only the mucus from an old-age infection, stuck there in the corner at the bridge of his nose.

His name is Herbert Washington, and he tells anyone who will listen, myself included, that he has lived in this part of town since he was a boy—not as uncommon here as it may seem in this modern era of mobility and transitory lives. He has seen men come and seen men go. He has seen things change.

"But of course not fast enough," he once said to me.

He stopped to remember. Then he frowned.

"Some things, I'd say, have changed a little too fast," he declared. "Some of the changes, I guess, we just weren't ready for; they caught us off guard. Some of the changes just never should have happened. We'd be a lot better off, I think, if some of the old ways had been left alone. I don't know much, but I do know this: things ain't supposed to be like they are. Things ain't like they used to be, that's for sure, and not what they could be, and not what they ought to be. But no matter how you look at it, things sure ain't supposed to be like this."

He shook his head and pocketed the handkerchief.

"Kind of makes you sad, don't it?" he said. He looked sharply in my direction, caught my eye and held my gaze for a long long time.

"And if it doesn't," he said, "it ought to."

He knew, he would often say, exactly what is wrong and exactly how to fix it, but whenever I asked him, he would always tell me the same thing.

It was an almost daily occurrence now, almost like a ritual. I would pass. Herbert would be standing as if on guard in front of his building. Our eyes would meet, our hearts shake hands, but instead of hellos, we would exchange greetings of a coded kind.

"Tell me what you know."

"Not today," Herbert would say. "You ain't been here long enough."

We would swap smiles. If I was actually going somewhere, I would continue on. If I wasn't in a hurry, which was most of the time, I would stop and we would chat.

The first time Herbert said this to me, that I hadn't been in Harlem long enough, I was shocked and nearly offended.

"Almost a year," I roared, for that was how long I had been here then. "Almost a year, and that's not long enough?"

"Not nearly long enough," Herbert would tell me again and again. "A year ain't nothing."

Once he even said to me, changing the daily ritual slightly but profoundly, and saying it as if he had given it a lot of thought: "A year ain't much; not if you're trying to learn about something more than yourself. And even then it ain't much."

For two seconds I said nothing. Those two seconds' hesitation probably told him everything he needed to know.

"You've been black all your life," he said. "Have you learned what that's all about yet?"

I said nothing.

He smiled then that imperceptible smile of a stud poker player who has aces wired back to back and knows you can't beat him and knows you can't drop out of the hand. All you can do is call.

Again I said nothing.

"No," he said. "You can't know either one in just a year. It's a lifetime of knowing, a lifetime of feeling. You got to know yourself a whole lot better, just like you got to know Harlem a whole lot better before you'll even know what I'm talking about. You can't be just living on the surface all the time. You got to get under it. You got to go through the changes, be here when summer turns to fall and winter becomes spring. You got to be here, you got to be in it. You got to blend in with these surroundings, see the way things are done here and be part of it all. You got to know your neighbors, and they got to know you, they got to see you, they got to get used to seeing you. You got to feel what's wrong with this place before you can know—before you can really know—what is good here and what is right. You got to know what's wrong with something before you can try to fix it, and what's right so you can leave that part alone. The answers are not as tough as you might think, and I'll tell them to you when you're ready. Believe me, I know what needs to be done."

Oddly enough, I did believe him, and I longed for Herbert to tell me what he knew.

What he knew, he said, no one else wanted to hear.

I guess that included me too. I certainly had my own notions about what I did and did not know—if not about Harlem, then at least about myself, the changes I had already been through, the seasons that had come and gone, and certainly what it meant to me at any rate to be black.

He was right about one thing. I did not want to listen to some old man who thought he knew better than I knew myself why I had wanted to come here, why I had needed to come here, and—he even said this—why I *had* to come here. But I did want to hear what he knew about other things.

What Herbert knew, he said, was that no one on these mean streets of Harlem would listen to him nor do what he would say to do.

"Who of these young people wants to hear what an old

man has to say?" he asked. "They all got more important things to do."

He grinned, but just a little. Then the grin became a smirk.

Your eyes follow his gaze as he glances around. You try to see what Herbert sees.

You look down the block. You walk this street, or any street, any avenue in Harlem, especially in summer, but anytime the weather is nice, and what you see will be the things that Herbert sees, the things that I saw—clusters of people; children playing on the sidewalks and in the streets; young women gathering, gabbing, women far too young to have so many babies at their feet, in their arms, held on out-thrust hips, pushed in flimsy strollers; young men huddling, posturing, and talking loud, pretending to fight; far more men than women. They get together each day, stand around and talk.

Herbert is one of them. He stands this day where he stands every day. He has nothing else to do, no place else to go. He takes his position early and stands here most of the morning. He talks to the old people who pass. He speaks to the neighbors he knows. He is not unlike the other men standing on these corners, in front of these buildings, sitting on stoops, hanging out in front of the little grocery shops. The one difference, though, is that Herbert is not young. Though he doesn't altogether look it, he is seventy-six years old.

"I've lived my life," he says with a certain pride, as if achieving a certain age were achievement enough.

"And I worked hard, very hard," he tells me, his pride in

himself and in what he has done showing itself all at once and then swelling. "I worked for everything I've got, and nobody gave me nothing." He tries to stand a tiny bit taller.

"I've made my living and all the noise I'm going to make. If I was going to have any kind of impact on the world around me, by now I would have already done it. Ain't much else I can do now. So I've earned this here spot and this nothing I do all day. But the young men you see up and down this street here, this is what they do. This is all they do. They got nothing else."

He tosses his head at the men on the next corner and sneers at them as if it was all their fault, and their fault alone. No one who sees him pays him any attention.

"It was never like this before," he says. "There was a time when an old man was respected and listened to, a time when people said 'Yes, sir' to you and 'No, sir'; 'Yes, ma'am' and 'No, ma'am.' They didn't do everything you told them to, but at least they would listen to you. Maybe we need to get back to some of that."

Herbert shrugged and slowly turned, moving back to lean against the wall of the building he lived in.

"Naw, it didn't used to be like this at all," he said. "But this is what it has all come down to now. Too many young men with no jobs, no prospects, no real way to take care of their responsibilities, not a damn thing to do but loiter on these streets all day and drink and do drugs, talk shit and make a whole lot of noise. Yeah, and make a whole lot of babies they can't take care of. Or don't want to take care of."

Suddenly his entire countenance changes. It is as if he

has grown tired and can no longer hold himself so erect. The frown remains, but his stern squint is no longer so severe, neither piercing nor accusing. His hand once again wipes at his eye as if to clear away a tear, and he mutters behind the handkerchief that hides his face.

"Poor forgotten children of God," he says, as if to himself, and you don't know if the old man is talking about the babies themselves or about the ones who make them.

As he speaks, as he wipes his eyes, you try to see what he sees, try to know what he knows and feel what he feels, and suddenly things are just a little bit clearer.

The twinge returns, the little pang at the back of my heart. I had felt it on the corner of Seventh Avenue and 135th Street, a small pain still throbbing as if from a scar that has not healed. I have felt it often, and I know for sure now it is the same ache I felt when I was a little boy and I watched Johnny Cannon do his stabbing. It is what I feel when I think of Pig Foot Mary.

It is a twofold feeling, two-pronged, for it pricks twice at once. It touches two nerves that are connected and yet somehow opposite, and when I stand where I stand I am tugged in two directions.

Herbert Washington takes his position and stands the same as he stands every day on this corner. He shakes his head time after time at the blight that further decays around him. He sneers at the young women with so many babies. He despises the young men with nothing to do all day but stand on these corners and bluster.

"They have no jobs," he says. "And that's one thing. But they have no initiative either. If they did, things wouldn't be

119

what they are. If they had some initiative, things maybe could get a little bit better."

It is for this that he blames them.

Somewhere between his anger and disgust, he hangs his head and wipes his eyes.

Seventy-five years ago, Herbert was just a baby. Harlem was new and alive. Harlem was magical. Seventy-five years later Herbert stands on a street corner and shakes his head in disgust. He has seen both sides of paradise. Now, he says, when he looks at Harlem and at what it has become, it makes him want to cry. Although he knows what to do to put things right, still, he says, he cannot understand what really went wrong.

He gets a faraway look in his eye. He shakes his head. It is—the same as everything is—not as it should be, and it makes you more than wonder. It can make you sad if you think about it. Or it makes you open your eyes and question. Always the how. Always the why. Always the what-ifs.

My father had that same faraway look in his eye as we drove home.

We spent most of that afternoon and evening without saying much. It is often that way with us. We have so little in common, it seems on the surface, that there is little for us to talk about. We often find ourselves manufacturing conversation, talking about events in the news, then easing gently into some kind of reminiscence. There is always my childhood, always my father's early life with my mother, always his earlier life before he knew her. I am like a small child: *Tell me about before I was born.* He has always been a storyteller.

He likes to tell me his truest stories. He likes to tell me how it was and how it is. He likes to tell me, too, how he thinks things ought to be.

Because I masquerade as a writer, this old man sees me, I think, as his witness, someone who will record the things he tells me and not let them die. It isn't simply that he wants me to know the deeds he's done. He wants me to know why he did them.

I don't think I ever understood this before today.

This is the only way he has, I guess, for me to know who he is and who he was and what he did to smooth for me the path I am on. Much of what he did was done so I wouldn't have to do the same, and much was done so that I could be not only who I am and what I am but, within reason, *any damned thing*, in my father's words, *I wanted to be.* He did what he did so that I could live the life I chose. He did what he did so that I could live.

All the things he did for me I will never know, but everything he did was right there, all of it, in his face as we drove toward home that afternoon and evening.

I have seen him with the look of a demon in his face, and he will stare at me sometimes as a gambler stares at the roulette wheel. He has borrowed against the future, mortgaged the house, sold pieces of his soul to place this wager, and everything—absolutely everything—is riding on this turn of the wheel.

Sometimes it is a softer stare he offers, and in his face is pure expectancy—which is different from the tense nail-biting expression of a gambler making his last double-or-nothing bet. This look in his face is all hope and all trust. It is the radiant gaze reserved for that god in whom all faith and all future reside, and for the sake of whom the many sacrifices have been made.

I am the culmination of my father's hopes and his efforts. I am somehow what he wanted to be. I am what my brother was before me and what no one else can ever be until I have children of my own onto whom I can pass this burden. I am, in the words of my father, *"the last of the big boys."*

I have been hearing this funny little phrase of my father's since I was very little. Often it was the ribbon on a package of praise. Often it was the stinging cattle prod of encouragement. Often it expressed disappointment at some foolishness or failure. Always it served to remind me that something was expected of me. I'm not sure I ever knew what it was, but I definitely knew it was something.

I knew it was something.

But there was in his face as we drove toward home something that I had never seen before. In his face was a look of deep sorrow and disappointment. In his face was the faraway look of fatigue that is born of loss and profound confusion.

He was lost in thought, and I didn't want to disturb him.

We had driven for over seven hours without saying much except to comment on the number of deer browsing at the side of the road. As we crossed into Ohio, a doe jumped onto the highway. We swerved and missed it.

"I've never seen so many before," he said.

He leaned forward and looked up at the sky through the front windshield.

"It's going to be a clear night," he said. "The moon is going to be bright."

He was right about the night sky. It had started to get dark. A few stars had appeared. There was not a cloud anywhere. But the moon hadn't risen yet.

"The deer come out in numbers when the moon is full, or nearly full, and very bright," he said. "So take it easy. You don't want to hit one of those things. And stop when you want to. When you get tired, let's get a hotel."

But I wasn't tired. My mind was racing two miles a minute. Harlem was in my head, my father was in my head, past and future were in my head. I wasn't worried about deer or about being tired. I just wanted the easy concentration that comes when you drive long distances. After a while you find yourself in a blank zone. Your mind runs on automatic. Thoughts and feelings come to you from nowhere, without order and without conscious connection. Time and distance pass unrecorded. Hours are consumed with a single thought. You don't remember covering the last seventy miles. You are only what you are thinking. Your body has become weightless and has disappeared. You don't feel the pain in your back or the stiffness in your legs until you stop for gas and get out of the car to stretch.

It was after midnight now. We were somewhere in Indiana. I was getting very tired, but we were only four hours from home and I didn't want to stop. My father had begun to talk. We had lived for a time in Indianapolis, and anytime he has an excuse, like being someplace he used to live, he starts remembering when, going back to that place when he was young and thin and happy to live in a one-room apartment and own nothing.

He was laughing, as he always does. The stories he tells, even when they are sad and serious, echo with joy and hilarity.

One minute he was climbing into the window of his girlfriend's house. Her parents were home. They got caught, and my father was scrambling back through the window.

The very next minute he was a taxi driver taking out-of-towners on a forty-minute ride to a place they could have walked in fifteen. But they wised up and refused to pay. My father pulled a pistol and shot it into the nighttime sky.

"You should have seen them as they ran away," he said. "They were running in zigzags down the middle of the street, screaming and shouting and throwing money every which way. Of course it was too dark for me to find it, but man! those were the days."

Those were the days, all right, and those are the stories he tells that I might know how great those days were. Many of the tales I have heard four thousand times by now. Some I've only heard a couple of hundred. But they never cease to be funny, and when this old man dies, his laughter and his weird stories are what I will remember most.

Suddenly the thought of his dying filled the car and fouled the air. We had driven into a strange mist, and things got a little spooky. The air outside had cooled off instantly and quite a lot. Now the hot breath of our laughter fogged the inside windows. I looked at him and he looked at me, and nothing was funny anymore.

It was my fault, I'm sure. I was wondering how he would

really like to be remembered: as a maniac laughing and full of life and telling his crazy stories, or as the old man he has become who sleeps a lot and drinks a lot. I would like to think of him as both of these, but also remember the man who reads a lot, a dictionary always at hand and still asking me definitions of words he has just looked up, as if I'm being quizzed.

He is, of course, all these and more, and I guess I'll never really know him, nor fathom entirely what he and other men and women like him did to smooth this bumpy ride we're on, but Harlem was on my mind at the moment and all I could think of was the sorrow in my father's eyes as he looked over what has become of the black world that used to be full of so much life and laughter and hope.

I thought then of the young man my father used to be, scuffling to take care of a family, missing out on all he could have had and done.

I was thinking of the man who always had two jobs when my brother and I were growing up. Sometimes he tried to work three. It meant we didn't get to see him much, which was all right with Tommy and me. My father was the discipline master in that house, and the less we saw of him the better.

It wasn't so hard on my mother. She was in on the plan, and anyway she had us in the same way that we had her always there. Not so with my father. It was one of those things he had to do, but I know now that it was hell on him not being with his family all the time. He was hardly home and didn't get to know my brother and me the way he would have liked. Nor did we get to know him very well.

I may never get to know him now as well as he or I would like, but I spend as much time with him as I can, and certainly I see him a little bit better now. I'll remember him differently too.

"Pop," I said. "What do you think? Any regrets?"

His expression was not quite the demon one. It was mostly hidden, barely illuminated by the dashboard lights and the lights from passing cars, but I could see he was looking at me like I had just said the stupidest thing he had ever heard.

"Brother," he said. "If you don't have regrets, then you never made any of the tough choices."

I have never thought of my father as particularly sensitive or thoughtful. I think I have been wrong.

"There was a time when I didn't have a care in the world," he said. "I had a job, a pension coming one of these days, and I had a car. That was good enough for me. I didn't want anything else, I didn't need anything else. Life was good to me, and I was having a good time."

He didn't need to say more. I knew what happened next. My mother came along and put a monkey wrench into the works.

"It's a whole lot different when you're not thinking just about yourself anymore. Suddenly you've got the future on your mind, and you've got to lay tracks to get there. That's what your mother was good at. We wouldn't have what we have if it weren't for her."

I hesitated to ask him this next question. I was afraid of the answer.

"Yeah, but, Pop," I finally said. "Have you been happy? Has it been worth it?"

"Happiness is not all it's cracked up to be. Don't forget that," he said. "You can enrich yourself with misery too, you know. So you make your choices and you stick by them. Then you try to find some happiness if you can. I've been lucky. I've had more than most."

"So it's been worth it," I said.

"I don't know," he said. "You'll have to answer that one. The world I'm leaving you is certainly not what anybody had in mind. We thought we were doing what was going to work out best. Sometimes it seems like just the opposite."

"We're doing all right," I said.

"Yeah, *we* are," he said. "And that's exactly why we did everything the way we did it. And maybe that's part of our problem. We did what we did, and we thought everything was going to keep getting better and better. But it didn't. Somewhere along the way we hit a wall. Somewhere along the way something happened, and I don't know if we walked to the cliff and got pushed or if we were led there and jumped. But I have the nasty feeling that whatever happened, we did it to ourselves. And if we didn't do it all, we sure helped."

*R*ight away I recognized the expression that had darkened my father's face. It was almost the same look, only more sinister, a puppy offers when he knows he's done something wrong but doesn't know exactly what. It resides halfway between sorrow and disappointment on the one axis, acceptance and something like—but not quite—relief on the other. Oddly, it is a look that I have seen many times in men's faces and that I myself have worn and that reminds me—now as I write, but not then during the night drive home—exactly why I had to come to live in Harlem. (*Had* to come to live here. More than wanted to, stronger than needed to, but, just as Herbert Washington suggested, *had* to—though not for the same reasons he would suggest.)

I tell myself, I told my father that night in the car when he finally asked me, that there are myriad reasons to come here, to live here, to be here, so many reasons that they jumble now into confusion, all of them true yet none of them quite complete. But there is only one reason I *had* to come.

To these "myriad reasons" my father responded, "Yeah? Like what?"

The only one that spilled from my mouth was that I thought I needed the experience.

I didn't know what else to say to him. I tried to find a suitable answer, one that would make sense, but it was all I could come up with. My thoughts were clouded with my father's expression, with Harlem's history, with Pig Foot Mary.

I stammered once and repeated. "Just to have the experience," I said.

My father said, "Hmm."

The experience I claimed to need and seek is, I suppose, the black experience, and although in many ways I have missed out on it, I have not missed it—for how can you miss what you have not had, what you have not known in such a long time? How can you say you miss what you have not wanted?

When I think back on Johnny Cannon and his stabbing victim, when I look out my front room window and watch a black man beating a black woman, when I think of the villain who broke into my apartment last year, I tell myself, Yes: I have not wanted it; I have not missed it.

I am telling the truth. At the same time, I'm telling a lie.

I was lying too when I told myself I thought my coming to Harlem was part of a logical progression, an evolution. When asked later why Harlem, I would often answer that Harlem was the next obvious place for me. After Africa and after the Deep South, Harlem was the only place that made sense.

Of course it could have been that after all this time I really did want simply and suddenly to be black—in ways that I had not been black before, or at least not in a very long time. It could be said too that I wanted to be poor for a while, that I wanted to limit myself so that I might know how the caged bird really feels.

I like to think of myself as living very often a life outside of my own, a life of others. As I did when I was a child pretending to be first one somebody and then another, I like to imagine myself in someone else's shoes, someone else's near-situation with the hope that I can see other sides of life, hear other stories, and understand other ways of being. Then I can know a little of how it feels, as nearly as possible, to be someone else. If I can put myself—or nearly put myself—in someone else's place for a while, having seen what he sees every day and having known the tiniest bit of what she knows and having felt a little of what they feel in their bones, perhaps when I see these others I can see myself.

We who live beyond the periphery of places like this need to be reminded that other worlds and other people exist. We who have seen these other worlds and lived in them will carry them with us everywhere and forever afterward. How much easier it is to remember them once we have met them, once we have lived among them, once we have laughed with them, cried with them, and tasted their tears.

Then even from a distance their smiles can be seen in the memory of our hearts.

Then even from a distance we can care about them.

I was not thinking of saving the world. I was only trying to save my own poor soul.

I was thinking of Pig Foot Mary Harris and how she made her fortune and got out of Harlem, and yet still managed to make money from those she left behind.

My father asked me that night in the car if I would be doing what I do and what I have done if I were not black. I didn't answer him.

I was thinking of Michael Simms, who had been my best friend in childhood before my father moved our family to the suburbs. I have missed Michael very much over the years and have longed often for his company and for his mother's cooking.

I was thinking of downtown landlords who stay away from Harlem, who take money out of Harlem and in a way suck the life out of it.

I was thinking of how the garden turned into rubble, how the flowers turned to weeds, how the mecca became a slum.

I was thinking of my father wanting to move to the suburbs.

I was thinking about what he said: that whatever has happened here, we did it to ourselves, and that even if we didn't do it all, we certainly had a hand in it.

I was thinking that by moving his family away from the black community, he was responsible—or felt he was.

I was thinking too much, and my thoughts were a cloud. I wasn't concentrating on my driving. I was no longer listening to my father. I heard him, but I didn't know what he was saying. I was getting sleepy, dreaming a little, dozing at the wheel. My head bobbing snapped me awake. It was the only thing that kept my eyes open.

Then out of the corner of my eye I saw it. Great brown eyes bulging in panic. A moment of gray caught in the headlights.

I heard the scream before I heard the impact, didn't know the scream was my own. The scream, more like a grunt, came after the thud, came after my life flashed before my eyes, not as a prelude to death but in answer to my father's unlikely question. I didn't realize I had heard it, but at the very moment we were slamming into a deer as it tried to cross the highway, my father was asking me: "Do you ever regret the life you've lived?"

Personne n'a le droit d'être heureux tout seul.

No one has the right to be happy all by himself.

—Raoul Follereau

To come home after a long time away is to feel the heaviness of a place's history, the weight of time that has passed, of the yesterdays you have missed. Even if the hands don't tremble, even if the knees don't weaken, there is a certain anticipation that feels a little like dread, a little like relief, and that stokes the imagination. Trepidation mingles with delight. A fire built of questions burns beneath your skin. Nostalgia moistens the eye, quickens the heart. There is triumph and there is doubt, and a vague sense of sorrow shapes your smiles as you make your way back home. Slowly—slowly the significance sinks in.

The significance has as much to do with the setting as it does with the actual return, for here suddenly before you is this place that is indeed home—or used to be—but that now is foreign ground. You know it, but you don't. It has made you, shaped you, gone with you from here to there, this place called home, fueled your dreams, warmed your thoughts. Wherever you roamed, you carried home inside, the way a warrior off to battle carries home and family and friends. But when you left it, you really left it. You left it all behind. You were not here when yesterday became today. You were not here to know it.

To be part of a place—any place—and to know it, you have to be there. As Herbert Washington says, you have to see the seasons change.

Here beside you now stands the sibling whose pulse beats in unison with your own, whose blood is similar to the blood that fills your heart, whose past is very much *your* past but whose history now is not your own. This avenue we travel is not a two-way street. Its single track leads instead to a fork in the road, which leads to a fork in the road, which leads to yet another fork. Where once there might have been one story, two histories and more diverge.

The markings are somewhat the same. The influences that frame your place in the world are similar to those that shape the world of the ones who stayed. That much is easy to see, and if you walk backward along your path you will find where your road meets these other roads; retrace further, and you will find the starting point. It is this place, the starting point, that once was home, and would be still if you had stayed, but that you don't know anymore—no, not fully—and that doesn't know you.

We pretend. We hope. We dream. No matter. It is no longer home.

And yet many many things are as familiar as if they were yesterday, so familiar they seem right; so familiar they seem good.

These are what we take along when we leave a place. They soften the smiles of strangers in strange lands; they make tolerable their ways. They warm the cold nights. These are the things that remind us of home and how it all used to be here. And these are the things that one day call us back. And when at last we see them once more, that's how we know we have come home again.

My memory is crowded with these markers of Harlem, these things I have done without, that I once turned my back on, that I have missed without realizing. They are what I remember from a time long ago when being black seemed a very fine way to be. It seemed, in fact, when I watched my father, that being black was indeed a lot of fun. It was hard work; it has always been hard work, but the task at hand gave us something to rally around, to close ranks against. It made the music louder. It made the laughter richer. There was nothing wrong then with living in a black neighborhood. Anyway, we had no choice. And anyway, we kept the neighborhoods mostly safe. And anyway, that's how I remember it. But then again, I left a long time ago, and I was very young.

I remember, I remember, I remember.

When I walk the streets of Harlem now, having moved, in a way, back home, I am flooded with memories of my youth, as if I were an old man. That is one of the great powers of place: to get you thinking, to get you feeling.

There are the obvious things, of course: friends not quite forgotten and food that has been replaced with more elegant fare but that now seems to taste even better than I recall, better after a few nights, I guess, in memory's cooler. I never knew how much I loved sweet potato pie until I came to live in Harlem, or how much I missed black-eyed peas and candied yams. We ate these things often when I was a kid, but we ate them, I thought, because we had to, because we were not the wealthiest folks on the block and eating a mountain of beans each week or two tons of collard greens was how to stretch the money. Nowadays, when I don't feel like cooking, I often wander over to Sylvia's on Lenox Avenue to stuff myself with what have become in my mind the delicacies of my youth. They don't do them as well there as Michael Simms's mother did them and probably still does them, but they remind me, as they are supposed to do, of what I have been missing. They remind me that I have been away and that I have come home.

All of a sudden nostalgia fills the blank spots in a memory, and no matter how good that food and those days really were, now of course everything *then* seems somehow better than it was or more than it was—or even worse than it was, which in a nostalgic sense is still better. You are an old man remembering when, wondering where the good old days have gone.

You come out of Sylvia's with a belly full of nostalgia. You stand on a street corner and everything seems familiar. You're home at last. The realization brings a satisfied smile.

But something is not quite right. Something is so familiar it is disturbing, and that smile of recognition fades away.

There is something about the way American black men walk that marks them in the world—not all, but many. They move with a certain swagger, as if to be seen, as if to make known a presence: a sexiness, a strength, a fearlessness. I myself walk with this same show-offy walk; I don't think I do it consciously, but it must come from the same place in my being, for it speaks the same meaning: *Look at me, see me; I am here.* When I see other black men walk, I see myself.

And there is something about the music that pours from the windows of Harlem, fills the air, booms from the big boxes on street corners and from passing cars. It is not the same music I grew up with, not the music my father's age would want, but in a way his music and my music and this music are very much the same music. At times it has been joyful and sad, by turns proud and prayerful, now angry; all of it music that attempts to soothe a soul in anguish. And if the music has changed, it is because the souls themselves have changed, responding, as does the walk, as does the rich rich laughter, the loud talk, as do the backs that still bend and the tired black faces that have not changed much since I was young and probably even since my father was a boy, responding to a situation that likewise has not changed. And when you stand on a Harlem street corner, with your tummy filled with nostalgia, your eyes smiling remembrance and recognition, then you will see how much of this place has remained the same, how after all this time so much is so very familiar—too much, in fact—that it seems as if time has stood still.

While this may make home feel at first like home and seem all the more recognizable, it underscores—for me at least—how histories have diverged, even while remaining entwined, and how home has become an unfamiliar place.

It is no longer the world I know, not the life I now have gotten used to. It is not a place I would care to remain. It is far too bleak now.

As of the very day I moved into Harlem, out of a population of over 250 million Americans there were 31 million blacks who by statistical definition were that day and are still seven times more likely than whites in America to die by homicide, who are three times more likely to contract AIDS, who are twice as likely to live in central cities and four times more likely to be born out of wedlock. Compared to white Americans, blacks are half as likely to have college degrees and three times more likely to live in poverty, three times more likely to be unemployed, seven times more likely to serve time in prison. One out of every three black men in his twenties is in jail. As much as we hate to admit it and try to skirt the manifestly obvious, skin color counts for much in this country, and despite what I believed as a child, despite what I still naively hope, that I could be and can be anyone I choose to be, achieve anything I want badly enough, and live any life I very much desire, being black is defined by certain statistical realities and by the narrower realm of possibilities.

The median worth of black households in America on that day was $4,169; of white households, $43,279.

This is not an average. This is to say that half the white households in America have a net worth of over forty thousand dollars, and that half the black households in this country are worth less than four thousand.

Something seems to have gone horribly wrong. Things are definitely not as they ought to be, not what they could be.

Being black in America has always been a less than easy task. Although I myself have been extremely lucky, for some, perhaps for many or even most, being black never seems to get any easier. In many ways it has never been harder.

"That," said my friend Wilson Clark, "is because this is a different America than the one that pretends to believe in fairness and equality. This is the America that we in the outer world know nothing about, pretending even that it doesn't exist and that if it does exist, it exists the same way the prison world does: because of the poor choices of the inmates—because of something they did. They could, the thinking goes, have been anything they wanted, lived any life they wanted, but this life in one way or another is what they chose."

Wilson is right. People have often asked me why the people who live in Harlem, if life is as bad here as it seems, don't just move away from here—as if they could, as if they had someplace else to go, as if for most people in Harlem living here has been a choice.

For some people it *is* a choice. For me these days, and for Wilson Clark, who came, he said, driven here by that woman with the baby stroller on the A train. These were not his words, of course. He never saw her. He had not been on the subway with me that summer day, but when I told him how she looked, he knew without another word the panic that widened her eyes. He had seen it already a thousand times, he said, and that's why he had come to Harlem: to get away from it.

"To escape," he said. "To escape that look in white folks' eyes."

Like Olivia Maxwell in Chicago, and like myself, I

guess, though I never would have suspected it beforehand, Wilson Clark had fallen under the spell of Harlem and into the trap.

"I didn't realize it when I came," he said. "I was just so thrilled to be coming here and then to finally get here. Man, that's all I thought I needed was to get here. But now I know that when I let that look—*you* know that look—when I let that look finally get to me, drive me almost out of my mind, when I let that look force me to come to live in Harlem, now I know I was letting the white folks win. I was giving up the game. And I was letting my grandfather down."

We were sitting in a dark bar on 125th Street, just off the corner of Morningside Drive. From where we sat, even if we had sat by the window or if we had been outside, we couldn't see it—and if you didn't know it already, you wouldn't know it from where we were—but we were sitting in the shadow of Columbia University.

If you walk a little farther down Morningside you will come to a park that starts in the flats but then climbs up a towering hill. This park, this hill, is the beginning of a line that separates two worlds. At the top of this hill sits one of the mainstays of the one world, the Columbia University complex, which, along with the other institutions that buttress and buffer it—Barnard College, Teachers College, Jewish Theological Seminary—remains a constant reminder of the privilege and opportunity the one world dangles before but then ultimately denies this other world. Columbia University is in Harlem, on its westernmost edge but undeniably clustered well within the confines of the neighborhood.

Along this corridor, from 114th to 120th Streets, the two worlds come together in the same way that cultures meet in those buffer zones that separate border towns: softly, the one always vaguely aware of the other and yet in a way completely oblivious, for life goes on and the twain rarely meet; so close and yet so far apart they might as well be on different planets, so close that the spires of the Cathedral Church of Saint John the Divine, which sits high atop this hill, can be seen from the flatlands below wherever there is a gap in the tall buildings.

It is easy enough to walk there, into that world, to sit across from the cathedral and have a coffee or a pastry in the Hungarian café on Amsterdam Avenue, easy enough to pass through the heart of Columbia's campus and cross over from Amsterdam to Broadway, out of what seems the delirium and despair of Harlem, whose glory days have clearly passed, and into a world that is all hope and opportunity and pointed toward the future, a world linked as if by some magical pipeline to the City of Gold, the rest of Manhattan and the rest of the world, a pipeline that clearly doesn't open onto the rest of Harlem.

It is easy enough to go there and see what they have, those who have, and what they who have not are missing out on, the same as it would be easy enough for those others to come see what their brothers and sisters in Harlem are lacking. It is easier still to stay where you are and pretend not to know, pretend not to care.

As soft and flexible as it seems, the frontier is nonetheless a hard-edged line that segregates the two worlds. Whether these two worlds seem separated by the grassy knoll of Morningside Park or by the soft border of 110th Street, also called Cathedral Parkway, or by any other geographical boundary, they are separated as well by the rigid boundary line of color and money. They are two worlds so physically distinct and so separated—not just separate— that something as ubiquitous in the rest of Manhattan as a taxicab is essentially nonexistent in Harlem. South of Cathedral Parkway, the symbol of the city might easily be a tricolored flag: white of course, and green like money, and then yellow. The yellow would be the yellow of taxicabs.

Certainly there are taxis in Harlem. But as you go in either direction along any of the avenues—south or north, down toward paradise or uptown toward Harlem—the careful eye cannot help but notice the comings and goings of the yellow cabs, their existence on one side of the line and their mysterious disappearance on the other. They are replaced on the Harlem side of the line by what are called the gypsy cabs.

The line—the line—the line that separates, the line that isolates, the line that turns Harlem into the prison it has become.

If you stroll downtown from 133rd Street where I live or from higher up, you will cut across the dark heart of central Harlem, dark as dark can be, and on through the soft edge of Harlem to the border area where Harlem ends and the rest of Manhattan begins, that buffer zone where the one world meets the other, where there is spillage and there is seepage and you stand as if in two different worlds at the same time.

In the buffer zone there are black people and there are white people and there are the brown Hispanics who to the undiscerning eye can seem black or brown or even sometimes white, and who are regarded in much the same way— if not by themselves, then certainly by the outside eyes looking in—that blacks are. Harlem belongs to them too now, to the Cubans and to the Mexicans, to the Dominicans and the Puerto Ricans whose neighborhood was once the lower east end of Harlem but then spread along the southern rim and up the West Side. Now those edges have blurred. It is impossible to tell sometimes where black Harlem ends and Hispanic Harlem begins, and you are as likely to hear Spanish in many parts of Harlem as you are to hear English.

Harlem belongs to all of us now, these blacks and Hispanics who, though at odds with each other in many ways, share in many more ways the same circumstance and fate and isolation, the same restrictions imposed by place. They all live in this land beyond the buffer zone, and the demons within Harlem and the demons without that conspire to make black life the prison it has become in Harlem and to maintain this prison conspire as well to lay the same dark shroud over the lives and conditions of the Hispanics.

Antonio Morales, who lives in East Harlem, has come to recognize that in New York City, in all of America in fact, it matters very much whether you're black or white or Hispanic. In fact, he says, it's the only thing that really does matter.

"It is all about race in America," he says. "Makes no difference how they try to dance around it, it is all about race: what you are, what you get, what you don't get. And if you're black or Chicano or Puerto Rican, all you have to do is turn on the TV and see what you are never supposed to have. Oh, they want you to want it, all right, and they want you to think you're going to get it. They want you to think it's all there in front of you waiting for you to just grab it, that it's all in your reach, all in a day's honest work; all you have to do is play the game they want you to play and the way they want you to play it. That's what they want you to think. That way, when you don't get it, you know it's always something *you* did wrong that keeps you from getting in on the good shit. That way they can keep you dissatisfied with yourself, always down on yourself, always wanting something you ain't never going to have, and always thinking you're nobody 'cause you don't have it: that new Benz, that gold Rolex, that high-powered job. That way they can keep you down, that way they can keep you here, always dangling just enough of the good life and letting you taste just enough of it to keep you plugged in and keep you from tearing the shit down—not just this shit you see all around you here, but the whole shit. Which is what we need to do: burn it all down and start over. But they keep us from tearing down their shit because that's the shit they got us thinking we want, and if we burn all that shit down, we ain't never going to be able to get it. So we burn our own shit down instead, trash our own neighborhoods, and let everything fall apart. We don't care about nothing 'cause for the most part they keep us drugged and they keep us calm by letting us have a nice color TV—with cable, of course!—a nice car, and promises that if we're good little boys and girls and if we pull ourselves up by the bootstraps, we can enjoy a nice life too—not *as* nice, but a nice little life. In the meantime, those straps are attached to boots that are standing on our throats. They don't want us to have good jobs, or really anything decent at all. If they did, don't you know they could make jobs for us. They don't want us to be part of their world. And they don't want us living anywhere but here. This is what they really want us to have."

He makes a sweeping gesture with his left arm, for he has no right arm, and shows you the street he lives on.

"This is all they want us to have."

We walk together along the street he lives on, East 111th, back in the other direction along the next street, and up toward 114th and Malcolm X, where the Dominicans sit for hours and hours on folding chairs and play dominoes in the afternoon. Antonio goes there to play every now and again. But there is something else going on there too. Either it's some kind of illegal gambling, or it's drugs. Someone is always peeping out around the corner.

Did you see any cops in the subway? Or down the block? Any cops coming this way?

As we walk, Antonio stays to my left and a little in front as he points out the decay—as if it needed pointing out.

I realize, watching him, that if you just look at his walk, at the way he moves his body, if you could ignore the color of Antonio's skin, you would swear you were watching a black man walk. It is the same swagger, it shouts the same message: Look at me, notice me, I am here and I am a lion on these mean streets; don't fuck with me!

Someone, however, did. It's how Antonio lost his arm.

Antonio, like a lot of the fellows he knows, like a lot of fellows on the street for whom there are no good jobs, nor anything close to a decent job, and no way to afford what gets dangled before them—and before all the rest of us too, I suppose—as the sine qua non of wholeness and happiness, Antonio used to be in the drug trade. He was lucky; all he lost was a few years in jail and his right arm.

"It could have been worse," he says. After he thinks about that a few seconds, he says: "I don't know about that. Maybe dying is not so bad after all."

Many of his partners and competitors have died on the streets: overdosed, shot to death, pushed out of upper-story windows.

"I guess dying beats going to jail forever," he explains. "You get a little taste of what they say life is all about, you blow up big, and then you die while you're still whole, before they take away your manhood and your self-respect. It sure as hell beats this poverty shit."

Just before going to jail—the first time—Antonio was ambushed while he sat on the front stoop of his building, playing a few games of dominoes before dinner. He was shot several times, either by the police, some say, demanding more protection money, or else by rival drug dealers, or else by pistol-packing punks in the neighborhood jealous of the clothes and the cars and all the attention Antonio got. He wouldn't tell me how much money he had made and spent, but he said it was a lot.

"What do you do with that kind of money?" he said. "It's all in cash. You can't walk down to the bank with it and start buying savings bonds. They want to know where you got it. The tax people want to know. The stores, though, they don't care; they like your cash, even pretend to like you too. So you find ways to spend the money, stupid ways, the stupider the better: clothes, a couple of cars you don't need, some jewelry. And then you got to spread it around a little bit too, you know, trying to have a good time with your partners while the good times last, 'cause they don't come easy and they don't come often enough around here. It's amazing how many friends you get when you start tossing around cash, buying things for everybody. But let a man get shot a couple of times, lose an arm, go to jail, his income starts to fall off: man, people will desert you like a mother-fucker."

He takes a few deep breaths and blows them hard through his nose. Then he is quiet. The swagger in his walk is not so pronounced now. He doesn't rock so much from side to side. In his face there is a frown of confusion where there had been one of defiance. He reaches for the arm that is not there and squeezes the stub.

We walk over to Malcolm X without another word.

There is another drug dealer I know, he goes by the name Nicky-No-Arms. He won't talk about it, but he is reputed to have killed many men: those who got in his way, those who would not or could not pay what they owed him, those who jeopardized his reputation or put at risk his income. He has made much much money. He has spent just as much. And he has stayed many nights in jail. He lost his arms when rivals in a drug-turf war kidnapped him one afternoon, held him down, and whacked at him with axes. They hacked off his arms—above the elbows—to teach him a lesson. Nicky and his boys had encroached on their territory. It was not a thing to be done. Why they didn't just kill him, no one seems to know, but it didn't discourage him from the drug business. Now he is more feared than before. Now he has little left to lose. He wheels himself around the neighborhood as bold as you please in a specially rigged land cruiser that he can drive without the use of his arms.

And then there was Henry.

Henry hit the streets when he was thirteen years old, selling crack cocaine. His was the only income in a household of five. In their home there was no other man older than his thirteen years. His three younger brothers had three different fathers; none of the men lived with the boys and their mother, Jolene. She didn't work. Who would mind the kids? she asked me. So she stayed home, stayed on the phone most of the day, or in front of the television, and the only people on the block making money were the drug dealers on the corners.

Henry once said to me, "That's all we knew, man. We never saw anybody going outside the house to work. All the women in the neighborhood did was talk on the telephone or watch the TV or sit around out front on the stoops and complain about this and that. If they did anything at all, once in a while they cleaned the house. And the only men we ever saw with anything that even looked like a job were the crack dealers. And they were damn sure the only ones who had anything like clothes and cars and money. So what am I supposed to do? I'm thirteen years old, I'm the man of the house, and we got no food 'cause the food stamps only last us to the middle of the month. I want to be like a man, I want to take care of my family, and the only men out there working are working the streets. What would *you* do if this is all you know?"

You should have seen the way he talked to me, this now seventeen-year-old man, four-year veteran street-corner drug dealer. His arms flailed out wide, two at a time, one at a time, always back hard with a pop to the chest, one hand slapping his chest, one hand sailing out for emphasis. And he had that walk. They all have that walk.

He looked so tough in his NFL jacket and his overpriced basketball shoes, his trousers baggy in the butt and loose everywhere, a nine-millimeter pistol stuck in the elastic band of his underwear. He looked so tough, his face as tired already as an old man's. If you saw the two of us standing side by side, you would be hard pressed to say which of us was older. But he was just a kid. He should have been in school somewhere, or on some playground chasing a ball around.

"School!" he once shouted at me. "Man, this is the school. Here is where you learn what it's all about."

What it was all about, of course, was the money. Now there was food to eat, "all kinds of food," he said, "any kind of food you want, just go on up there and have my mamma fix something for you." He was the man in the house; he gave the orders now.

"She needs an old man like you around the house sometimes anyway," he said. It was good to see him laugh.

Upstairs in the crowded apartment there was too much bad furniture and not enough space. Two old sofas were jammed in a corner next to a small table. Flimsy kitchen chairs were in the living room. The walls were crowded with tasteless pictures, some religious, some political, some adverts cut out of magazines. And there was Jolene, not much more than a kid herself, just sitting around, exactly as Henry said she'd be.

She had Henry when she was fifteen—because she was in love, she said. Yeah, it was an accident, but "I wasn't thinking about giving up *my* baby. And Henry's father, his name was Henry too, he was a fine young thing. You could see he was going somewhere with *his* life. Well, he sure enough did. He got me pregnant with another baby, and then he went on about his business. Not another word out of him. Just gone. And the other two: that was just me being stupid, needing a man. One man already had a wife, and the other fool was just looking for somebody to fatback on— looking for somebody to take care of him. That got old quick, and I threw his ass on out of here." She snapped her fingers three times with a flourish.

She smoked a cigarette and chewed gum at the same time, both with an exaggerated relish. The long handle of a heavy plastic comb was stuck in the back of her hair. But just as Henry promised, she said she would cook lunch for me. She opened the cupboards and from among the stacks and stacks of cans and boxes of food, bags of chips, plastic bottles of colorful fruit-flavored drinks, she pulled out a can of Vienna sausages and a box of macaroni and cheese.

There was a small TV in the kitchen that she watched while she cooked—or rather, while she heated up the lunch. There was a larger TV in the living room too, only four feet away. It was on at the same time. She was watching two programs at once.

The floor was covered with basketball shoes. Jolene said Henry owned dozens of pairs, a different pair for every day of the month, and he gave his brothers, it seemed like, she said, a new pair each week.

"And why not?" she said. "He's making three, four, sometimes five thousand dollars a week. Bought himself a new car the other day. Says he's going to buy me one too— soon as I can learn to drive."

"And you don't care how he earns the money?" I asked her. She looked at me, cigarette dangling from her lip, like she hadn't heard, or like she thought I was crazy.

And why should she care? Perhaps a little for his safety on the streets, for young men die too easily on the streets and die too young, but certainly not for the illegality of his dealing, certainly not for the immorality of it. Not with this kind of temporary money at stake. And not with the permanent squalor she sees all around them every day. The money will come and the money will go, she knows, and life is a temporary thing; the lucky ones die young. But this despair goes on and on, so you take what you can while you can.

Henry slipped into the drug trade the same as most young people on the street. He went and talked to one of the dealers on a nearby corner. They're easy to find. They're all over the neighborhood. Anyway, Henry and everyone else knew all the dealers around, knew who they were and where they stood each day.

The dealers, of course, have no qualms about hiring a young boy of thirteen, or eleven, or eight—as long as the young boy buffers between the dealers and the police. And the younger the boy, the thinking on the street has it, the harder he works, because for the first time in his young life—and it may be for the only time in his life—he'll be respected. He's part of something, making his own money, doing for himself, and now he's got something to show for his time: money and the things money can buy.

"Most often," Antonio told me, "a boy starts as a kind of runner. He takes the buyer's money, goes to where the drugs are hidden, comes back and completes the sale. He doesn't have anything else to worry about, just taking the money and getting the drugs from where they're hidden. He's not supposed to concern himself with the police or guns or anything else. We got other people up and down the block whose job it is to watch out and protect the business. All he has to do is worry about his end, work an eight-hour day, get paid at the end of the week. It's just like a legit job, only easier."

"Except for the risk," I said.

"Except for the risk," he echoed. "But the bigger the risk . . . You know how that goes. Who can turn it down? I know I couldn't. Five hundred dollars a week. Easy money.

Six hundred dollars a week. It just gets easier. You get more responsibility, closer to the boys at the top of the ladder, you make more money. It's just like corporate America."

By the time Henry was fifteen years old he was handling twenty, twenty-five, thirty thousand dollars a week—not his own money, of course—all from the sales of small vials of crack cocaine, three dollars a hit.

"People would sometimes buy a hundred vials at a time," Henry told me. "And we're not just talking about people from the neighborhood. These are white boys from downtown, from Long Island, from Jersey. That's where the money is. And they come here to get what we got."

Not that people from the neighborhood weren't buying as well. Many women, young and not so young, always very thin and haggard, but always with the greatest smiles, have offered themselves to me for the meagerest amounts of money. And I have been told that the busiest day of the month for the dealers is the day the welfare checks arrive.

"And who is there to care?" Antonio asked. "Not the mothers of these young boys." He checked himself.

"Okay," he said. "Maybe some mothers care, if they know, because maybe they realize their sons are going to die or wind up in jail. Those are the only two places this road leads to. And they have to know that, if they know anything at all, if they even care at all. So they do what they can, I suppose, but what can you do with a young boy who thinks he's suddenly a man and he's making more money in a few weeks than you made all of last year—if you made any money at all apart from your welfare check? If you come down on him for what he's doing, he just moves out, moves in with his pregnant fifteen-year-old girlfriend and her mother, who are happy to have him and the clothes and the color TVs. And all that food and all that stuff he's buying just ends up in somebody else's house. And the somebody elses don't care at all where he gets the money or how he ends up. They don't care. They never do."

So the mothers often pretend they don't know what's going on, pretend they have no idea where all the sudden money comes from. They learn to stop asking.

"Everybody," Antonio says, "turns a blind eye—from the police on down: family, friends, people on the street. They just want to get from you while they can. Nobody really cares about you."

Jolene said she cared. She was worried about Henry's physical safety on the streets, but she was also worried about the spiritual death that haunts these streets. She had seen it grip the other boys in the neighborhood. She admitted it had even taken hold of her.

"But what can you do?" she griped. "What the hell choice do we have?"

The last time I went to see them, Henry had been shot dead. He was seventeen years old.

My father wants to know if I regret the life I have lived, wants to know too, I suppose, if I regret missing the life I never had. At first glance the answer seems a blatantly easy one to give.

My young friend Henry lies dead on a table in his living room. Someone has carried him home and has laid him here. The table is low, close to the floor, like a little altar, and is surrounded by the basketball shoes that are so adored in the neighborhood. They are strewn all around Henry's young body like some kind of offering, as if he had been a god. And for a little while Henry *was* a god, in this house, in this part of the neighborhood. His face had once shone with the pleasure of power and recognition. Now his eyes are like ice. They hold no look of shock or surprise at what has happened. The eyes have always known, even if Henry didn't, that it was only a matter of time. The eyes frown now not from wonder, and not from remorse, but as if in Henry's seventeen years they have seen far too much. His face has been battered tough, his eyes are tired beyond belief. It is a face already too old to be so young. But it will get no older.

In another part of Harlem, Nicky-No-Arms lies between two streams of blood spilling onto the cold concrete floor of a warehouse somewhere. He shivers but cannot hug himself for warmth or comfort.

The mother of Antonio Morales spreads her legs in the backseat of a car. Another baby is born in Harlem.

There is nothing prissy, nothing neat about these streets where I live. I walk them every day, I stand at my window. What I see tears at my eyes. What I feel exposes who I am.

Not so long ago, across the street from where I live, new neighbors moved in for a short time. I watched them off and on that evening for over two hours as they set up house, laid the table, and got the fire going for a barbecue. They cooked. The radio blasted until the batteries went dead. The children played.

I thought nothing of it. It was the beginning of my second winter in Harlem. By then I had seen plenty.

The air outside was cold and damp, but the fire in the barbecue glowed with heat, first red, then white. It was, all in all, a happy scene. The three adults sitting on folding lawn chairs told loud stories and laughed. The children shared laughter of their own. They jumped rope. They played tag. They argued the way children do when one of them doesn't get his way. Then they all sat down to eat.

Funny thing though: there is no building across the street from where I live. There is only a large parking lot. Behind the lot is a grassy incline, and behind the incline there is a new track and a football field built for the school that's just up the road. Surrounding it all, there is a stone fence with iron bars along the top to keep out intruders. In front of this fence, on the sidewalk, my new neighbors had set up house. Their moving van was a metal cart on long loan from a grocery store.

The children played between parked cars and in the street. Dinner was set up on cardboard boxes overturned. When they finished eating and it was time for bed, the children slept curled up on blankets laid on the pavement.

I thought absolutely nothing of it.

It rained during the night. In the morning the family was gone.

One evening not long afterward, three squad cars pulled up in front of my apartment building. A lot of commotion, a lot of noise. One cop stood outside. The other five stormed into the building. I leaned out the window and watched for a few minutes. Then I turned away. My biggest curiosity had been about the lady cop who was with them and why *she* had been the one to stand guard outside and not one of the men. I was curious too about my strange *lack* of curiosity.

A few months later, someone took a shot at me on the street. As I rode my motorcycle down Amsterdam Avenue, a young man in front of a corner store leveled his arm and followed me with the barrel of a pistol. He fired twice, I assume at me. I put on the gas and didn't look back. Neither did I even flinch.

It is amazing what you get used to. By now it was all seeming normal. I had come a long way from Johnny Cannon, but in fact not so long a way at all. It seems too often that not much has changed since then.

And my father asks if I regret this life that I have missed.

I shout my replies into each Harlem night.

Over and over I have told myself that none of this is really mine, that I have gotten away from here, that I have disconnected myself from this world, that I have in fact escaped. Even now on this return I knew I would not be here long and certainly not forever. (Or so I thought.) The world outside my window each day and every night, the world I visit when I walk these streets, the world of Johnny Cannon stabbing, of the man just below my window trying to beat the will out of this woman, of Henry, of Nicky-No-Arms, of Antonio Morales, these are all parts of the same world that I have for two years now been walking through. This is not the world I think of as mine. I am only a visitor here, only passing through until my time here is up, and then I can be gone again. Then this world will have disappeared once more from my life.

No! My world—or so I thought—the world my father had sought to give me, is a world far from this one. The world he wanted for me and the world I seem to have found is a world without Harlem's borders, without Harlem's limits. No, nothing so corny nor so unrealistic as a world where *"All God's children . . ."*—or any such nonsense—no, not yet, not in this time or place. My father is a crazy man, it is true, but he is not so naive as to believe yet in a world where black men are judged solely by the contents of their character. He has dreams aplenty, my father does; that one is not his. My father has always been a realist.

No. The world he wanted for me was a world where I would, anyway, be able to choose for myself, a world where I would have choice.

When I was a young teenager he took me once to see a movie at a theater in his old neighborhood. I think it was a theater called the Comet. In my father's day it had been a swank movie house, but a black movie house when places like the Fox Theatre, the Loew's State, and the Loew's Mid-City were off-limits to black people. They—the mysterious and ever-present *they*—didn't want black people enjoying the same as the white folks, couldn't have them in the same space, wanted of course their money and so had to give them someplace else to spend it. And so there were movie houses like the Comet and the Criterion that my father continued to go to even after blacks were finally allowed into palaces like the Fox—at first in the balconies, the Nigger Heavens, as they were called, and then finally in the main part of the theater, but not until it was clear that the neighborhood was becoming blacker and blacker and the white folks had started to flee to the suburbs, leaving behind the black folks and the expanding, ever-earthly Nigger Heaven.

Nigger Heaven. How does it sound? Not bad. Almost cute. Maybe in its day, even a little bit funny. It was what Carl Van Vechten called his novel about Harlem. It referred to those balconies where the black folks had to sit if they were allowed at all in white theaters, with the white folks occupying the good seats, the orchestra section below, "occasionally to turn their faces up toward us," my father told me, "their hard, cruel faces, to laugh at us or sneer at us, but they never beckoned us." In those old days when such terms could still be used, Nigger Heaven referred as well— and it still could—to uptown New York City, to Harlem. Places apart, Harlem and those black balconies: they were then, and they still are, all of them the same.

W. E. B. Du Bois, criticizing the Van Vechten novel, complained that " 'Nigger Heaven' does not mean . . . a *haven for Negroes—a city of refuge for dark and tired souls; it means in common parlance, a nasty, sordid corner into which black folk are herded, and yet a place which they in crass ignorance are fools enough to enjoy.*"

I asked my father why we still went to the Comet and to the Criterion when we didn't have to, and he looked at me for a long, long time.

"*You* don't have to," he said. "We've tried to make sure of that. But I still have to."

He could see, I suppose, that I didn't know quite what he was talking about.

"Sometimes," he said, "you have to do things you really don't have to do."

"How come?" I said. "If you don't have to do them, then you don't have to do them."

He smiled.

"Watch the movie," he said. Then he slouched down in his seat and went to sleep.

I still remember the movie we saw—or rather, that *I* saw. It has been since then one of my favorites, but at the time it was quite confusing: a convoluted Italian Western with American actors and a twisting story you had to follow carefully or it would lose you. My father, who had been drinking that day, gave up on it early and went to sleep. I watched the movie twice.

When he awoke he was sober, which was bad luck for me.

We had started the afternoon partying at my older sister Camilla's house. My father wanted to go to a movie, but of course we had to cruise through his old neighborhood first. He always took me along because he knew that at some point he would have a few drinks. Even though I was only thirteen years old, I already knew how to drive. My brother, who was fifteen, had been in no hurry to learn. I had always been my father's sidekick anyway; I became my father's backup partly by default. He knew I could always drive him home if he needed me to.

Unfortunately, he had sobered up. He always did, and I never got my big chance to drive the car all the way home.

Before we started out he turned to me and gave the look that has always reminded me and warned me at the same time that he expected much of me, that I, as "the last of the big boys," was and am the focal point of this man's dreams and of all his struggles.

"This world is a cruel and hostile place," he said as we drove toward home. It was not the first time I had heard it from him. "It will kick you in the ass if you let it." Then he gave me that look and commanded.

"Brother," he said, "don't you let it."

He spent the next half-hour telling me what a hard, cruel man he was—he liked the image he thought we had of him as a tough guy; he reinforced it whenever he could. He wanted me to know of the things he had done to keep the world from taking too big a bite out of his soul. He especially wanted me to know what he had done so the world would take an even smaller bite out of mine.

He said, "This world we're living in does not make a whole lot of sense. You will find very often in this crazy life that you have to do things you don't really have to do. And that's different from doing things you don't *want* to do. There is a consequence to everything; remember that. And you never have to do what you don't want to do as long as you're willing to pay the price of conviction. Do you understand?" I gave a little nod.

"But you *always* have to do what you *have* to do."

He smiled his moonbeam smile then, covering his mouth the way he always does when he laughs.

"Even," he said. "Even when you don't have to."

Then just as quickly, the smile was gone.

"Maybe especially when you don't really have to," he said. He was nodding to himself. He had found for himself a moment of clarity. He paused a moment to think it over.

"That's how you know," he said. "That's how you know who you are. That's how you know what's important to you. You've got to be your own man. You've got to create a world of your own, one that makes sense for you; that is one of the ways you do it.

"Always, always, always," he said, "look out for yourself and take care of your own. Everybody else is doing the same—no matter what you might hear. So try to create your own world and don't let anybody ever tell you who you are or how you ought to be; not even me. You be the one to decide."

Then that look again, and the question that was more a command.

"Do you hear me?"

"Yes, sir," I said. And we drove home.

Over and over I can tell myself, because of this man now grown old, because of the avenues he pointed out for me, that I am a prisoner neither of Harlem nor of the color of my skin. When I look around me now I see that the life I have lived has nothing in common—so I again tell myself—with the life Henry lived before he was killed. My world is a world far removed from the world of Nicky-No-Arms, of Antonio Morales, of the nameless others. I long ago escaped from the narrowness of that world and those lives.

In a way this world where I now find myself is my father's world more than it is mine. Oddly enough, this is not the world he wanted me to have.

"Yeah," he often told me. "It was good enough for me. It is *not* good enough for you. It is not *enough* for you. So don't you settle for it."

It seems very often that there are these two ways to be a father: either you want your sons to follow in your own sacred footsteps, or you want your sons to follow an easier path. My father worked hard to disinherit me.

Harlem was part of the world that was his. It was the world as he knew it: a hostile and bitter place with rigidly defined boundaries of where he could and could not go, what he could and could not do. It was a world he struggled most desperately for me to avoid.

Perhaps it was a world he himself would have wanted to escape, but being of another time and being too much a part of that world, too much a product of it, he was unable to pull completely away. He always had one foot stuck in that world's reality. The other foot he could—and did—lift out and set down in a world of dreams and possibility, but it was shaky ground, too unstable for him to get a foothold there and climb out onto. So instead, he lifted *me* up, carried me the way he did when I was an invalid child, and set me down in the world he wanted me to have, a place where the terrain was a little less harsh.

Perhaps there had been no choice for him. Perhaps he had to live in Harlem. But he made sure that I didn't have to, made sure I would not be confined to a life of hopeless resignation and gloom, some Nigger Heaven where the high walls of the labyrinth block out the beacons of possibility and choice and freedom, the maze where Antonio Morales lives, where young Henry died, and where Nicky-No-Arms rules the streets; this world where you can be shot at in passing just because your bike is blue.

None of this is to say that every square inch of Harlem is misery and surrender. Not very far, in fact, from where I live, there is a small two-block section of Harlem that in the glory days was called Strivers' Row. Two streets, 138th and 139th. Bounded at either end by Seventh and Eighth Avenues. Two blocks of row houses designed and built in the late 1800s by the famous architect Stanford White, some of them, and the others by Clarence S. Luce and Bruce Price. These homes were then among the most elegant buildings in Harlem. They still are. But the people who own them and who live in them seem to live a life apart from the rest of Harlem.

Built, of course, for white people and enormously expensive, these large and beautiful townhouses of brick and limestone were given up when the nature of Harlem changed. The white folks moved out. Black folks moved in. The section came to be known as Strivers' Row because of all the doctors, the lawyers, the members of the black elite, who lived there. They were the only black people rich enough to afford to live there. They were the strivers.

It might still be called Strivers' Row, and for the same reason. The price of these townhouses is more than the average Harlemite will see in a lifetime.

There are other elegant homes in Harlem, other fabulous and expensive townhouses, swank apartment buildings where doctors and lawyers and politicians hide behind doormen in uniform, private courtyards, and high prices. They live here still. They have stayed in Harlem. At the same time, they don't really live here. They don't see the same world the other Harlemites see. (But at least they are here; and that's something—I don't know what, but something—even if they live lives barely connected to the rest of Harlem.)

They send their children to private schools out of the neighborhood. They take vacations to Europe, to Africa, to

Polynesia. They come and go with the ease of a chauffeur-driven car. They do their shopping mostly away from the neighborhood. They are ambitious, still striving, still reaching—and prospering, it seems, even if their brethren are not.

Early on during my time in Harlem, when I still had a few dollars in the bank, I stood in line to draw money out of a cash machine. The woman in front of me was old and wore a fuzzy cloth coat that was frayed at the edges. She was short. I am not, and being more than curious, I peeped over her shoulder as she did whatever she was doing. When her bank balance flashed onto the screen of the money machine, I was astounded. She had close to twelve thousand dollars in her checking account.

There is money in Harlem. There is life in Harlem. There is ambition and success in Harlem. Unfortunately they are hidden. Because they are hidden, they cannot erase the images of Harlem that prevail: that of a tired and lifeless world overcome by violence and poverty and despair, where the exit routes are barred at every turn.

This world that is Harlem is not the world as I have come to know it, but it *is* the Harlem I have come to know. It is not the world I want.

Nor is it the world my father wanted for me, and for me to have answered him—*Do I regret the life I've lived?*—in any way but the way I did would have been to repudiate all he had ever done. I would have disappointed him, I am sure, the way Wilson Clark feels he has let his grandfather down, for my father sought to give me—and somehow succeeded—a life of choices where none had existed before, a life of advantage and wide possibilities.

So I offer my thanks and I shout my replies to my father's question into the darkness of each Harlem night.

But sometimes in the day I wonder as I walk. Sometimes I just don't know. Come then in those moments the fires inside that are built on a pyre of questions. First my father's questions. Then my own.

Do I regret the life I've lived, he wants to know; do I ever get the feeling that we've done everything all wrong?

When he asked, there was in his voice the same kind of liquid sadness that fills his eyes when he has looked for the old neighborhood and cannot find it, when he wonders what became of the world he knew, what became of the world he had hoped and worked for, what, in fact, has become of the world.

I don't know what happened to the world he had wanted to create. Maybe in some way I have actually managed to live it. I'm not sure. But the world he once knew, that world he sought to escape by moving to the suburbs, was in many ways right here in Harlem, right here on these streets, right here outside my window.

Not much has changed in the time since I've been gone. And yet nothing seems the same.

I feel sometimes like my father must feel when he goes searching for the old neighborhood. It seems, when I look for it, that too much from the old days that was good has gone, and I recognize little. I feel lost. I feel a little sad. Those things that were not so good have gone nowhere. So much that ought to have changed has remained the same. Johnny Cannon is still in plain view when I look out my window.

The wisdom of Herbert Washington rises to me in those moments, and I hear him tell me once again that some things have changed too much and far too fast; others not fast enough. Those things that have not changed cause for me the most bewilderment. I don't know if my father feels this too, but I am in a time warp, and there is an odd discomfort at finding what is familiar.

The world should have moved on by now. Nothing should be as it was. But it is. Time has stood still, has even, in many ways, gone backward.

Strivers' Row notwithstanding, there are too many faces imprisoned in Harlem, too many backs bent from bearing a load that does not go away at the end of the workday or week, too many souls atrophying from the effects of hopelessness, too many eyes glazed over from narcotics numbing the effect of not enough chances, of being pushed to the edges and left there, discarded and uncared-for, on the trash heap of Harlem.

For many of the people of Harlem everything is the same as it was. Yet nothing is the same. Maybe I and the life I've lived are evidence.

But sometimes I wonder. Sometimes I am racked with guilt. Perhaps my father too. Perhaps it is why he wants to know.

The night he asked had been a very clear night, exceedingly starry, surprisingly cold, and we stood shivering side by side, each of us silently and in his own way thinking about the wreckage that lay before us.

"We have been very lucky," my father said. "It's enough to make you wonder."

"Wonder what, Pop?"

"I don't know," he said, fumbling now lest I suddenly discover this side of him he thinks he has kept hidden. "Maybe I'm wondering why some people and not some others."

"Yeah," I said. That's all I could think to say.

I looked from one to the other, from the wrecked car to the deer lying dead in the road.

I wanted to say something philosophical. My father spoke first, saying something then that seemed silly, given the direction the conversation was taking, but more like the man I knew.

"Brother," he said. "It is sure a pity to waste all that fresh meat."

Immediately, a semi truck came roaring down the highway and ran over the carcass, no longer meat, just mush.

I glanced sideways at my father. He was shaking his head. He still couldn't get over how lucky we had been.

We walked up to a gasoline station in Pocahontas, and while we waited for the police and a tow truck to come, the gas station man filled my father's ear with stories of similar accidents, one where the deer instead of being hit straight on, the way we had done it, had come up over the top of the car, crashed through the front window, and as it was trapped but not dead yet, started kicking frantically, trying to break free. The deer ripped open the chest of the man who had been driving the car.

"They get crazy when they get trapped like that," the man said.

My father trembled a little and frowned.

Now suddenly I heard the question for the first time. I don't know why—maybe the fragility of life suddenly made all too clear, maybe the thought of being trapped myself, I who so far had been so free, I believed, and knowing how crazy I would get if I were ever similarly trapped—don't know why it hit me then, but it did.

I realized now that I had heard it as we were hitting the deer. I realized too that in the instant of the accident I had seen selected glimpses of my life flashing in front of me.

These flashes came not accompanying death, as myth says they will. They came as part of the question I was only now conscious of having heard. They came as part of the answer.

From the flashes you start to grab randomly, close events first, then ones from farther away. You start to play silly scenarios in your head, a game of what-ifs. What if we had gotten a hotel in Columbus and had slept away the rest of this night? What if we had been driving a little faster? A little slower? What if we had been five miles—or more— from the nearest town instead of five minutes?

What if when I was ten years old I hadn't kicked Donna Quirk in the thigh for ripping up a paper airplane I had just made; what if I hadn't gotten into so much trouble that day? She was a white girl. It was a mostly white school. What if the trouble had been worse?

What if I had married my college sweetheart? She was a white girl. What if her family hadn't raised such a ruckus?

So many ways I could have avoided being on that road that night. So many little avenues, twists, and turnings that had put me there. So many reasons in fact that I had to be there—if only to hear my father's stories one more time. So many reasons for why Harlem, and why now.

And so many ways the accident could have been a disaster.

If I had never realized it before, if I never think the same way again, I knew all of a sudden that I had been blessed with a charmed life. There have been a multitude of missteps and mistakes, each one followed, it very often seems, by a miracle. I have walked a balancing act that leaves my fearless brother nervous and amazed. I have sinned and I have grieved for things I've done and I have wept at the loss of dear friends. Many things I wish I had never done, many things I wish I could do over. But after all the sorrows and all the triumphs, there is no one else or no way else I would rather be. And not a thing, nothing in this world, would I trade away for being in the car that night with my dear father.

To him who has heard me cuss only once before, and now twice, I said, "Hell no, Pop. I do *not* regret the life I have lived."

(But I should have said instead: I do not regret the life that you have given me.)

He looked at me with that strange expression he sometimes gets, as if he had no idea what I was talking about. In the excitement of a few perilous moments, it seems he had forgotten already that he had asked anything at all—or was pretending to. I, on the other hand, could not forget. The question was hot on my mind the rest of the night and the rest of that early morning, the rest of that day and every day in fact thereafter, always when I walked the streets of Harlem, and anytime I let my memory drift over the tour of duty I had done there.

The question and the answer were on my mind still two years later, when on another late night and early morning I looked from the window of my apartment and saw in the street below a man trying to beat submission into a woman.

It was Johnny Cannon all over again. We haven't come very far at all.

All this time I thought I had escaped, as if escape were ever possible, as if you can climb out of your skin, make a decision, and have it so. You believe somehow that by simply wanting a thing and by thinking a thing you can therefore have the thing. And then you wonder why others have not and cannot make the same decision, and why they cannot have the same things.

I got out; why can't they?

Why can't they?

Wait a second, wait a second!

Did I just say that?

I got out; why can't they?

There! That feeling was upon me that I now call the Pig Foot Mary twinge, only this time it was no twinge. This time it was a sharp stabbing pain, as if someone were kicking me hard in the ribs.

I was listening still to Antonio Morales as he led the way

to Malcolm X and 114th. "Yeah," he was saying. "We are some bad men." But instead I heard myself speaking. *I got out; why can't they?*

I sounded like an ex-friend of mine who has said to me many times: "I did it. Why can't they?" She had not been talking about escaping from Harlem, but she might easily have been—if she had been black—and I sounded just like her.

Worse, though: I thought I sounded too much like the old lady in Cleveland who, having read my previous book, wrote me this letter:

I am a white woman, 70 years of age. I read your book to try & understand your race better. I was raised in the north but spent 2½ yrs in the deep south with my husband during W.W.II. He was in the service. I was Catholic & lived (room and board) with many families & never had a problem. I didn't try to *convert* anyone. To be accepted by *any group*, social etc you must be accepted first & conform . . . I live in an integrated neighborhood, been here 25 yrs. The blacks move here & bring the crime with them. An apartment at the corner sells out every three years & starts over again. Apts are destroyed, garbage in yard, kids out at all hours, loud music, drug dealing, drinking. Yes, we all know they (blacks) are in the neighborhood. You can see & hear them day and nite. Do I speak to them—NO. Why should I. I don't want to know this kind of inconsiderate neighbor who lowers property values. Why do blacks think we have to accept them, just because you're black. Your race has to *learn* to obey rules of society to be seen as civilized. Sure we fear you because you commit so many crimes & especially crimes against each other. Blacks are not safe in black neighborhoods. Why don't they improve a neighborhood instead of destroying it. The Blacks destroy their own back yard. Housing projects have been built & destroyed by themselves. They complain of garbage in yards—it's their own, not mine. Time & again the govt has tried to help. You must help yourselves. I am Irish & married an Italian when an Italian was one step above a nigger (50 yrs ago). I was considered a pig shit Irish (there were lace curtain Irish also). My husband was a dirty Guinea or dago. We raised 3 kids, *worked hard,* moved into neighborhoods, keep our property up, raised our kids to *respect* church, school & neighbors' rights & were always accepted because we were *assets* to the community *not liabilities.* People living today never owned slaves. Some today work as hard as slaves to survive. We still have "white trash" & hillbilly persons but many have worked hard & own homes & have moved up. There are others who will always remain white trash & feel sorry for themselves. The mines (coal) closed 50 years ago & they stay on welfare waiting for the mine to reopen. Public education is available to _all_. All you have to do is use it. I'm sure you received government loans for your education. It is available to all in need *if* you have maintained your grades. When my daughter planned on going to college (I & her father are 11 grade educated) she was required by law to have a foreign language, algebra, chemistry etc. We have lowered the standards for college entrance for blacks to be eligible. We have lowered the standards for high school graduation so more blacks can get a diploma. Welfare (up to now) has been expanded by President Johnson to fight the war on poverty. It has only been abused. *Everyone* has to work to better themselves, it can't be gotten by just *demanding* it. You cannot *demand* respect either—you earn it. I got your book at the library, so you make no money on me. If you've read this far maybe you will see the other side of how white people feel. Your people have been here longer than mine. You want it *all your way* instead of integrating into society. You want to take over. A civil war will again be fought in this country.

No name or address.
You might come & shoot me.

I might go and shoot her. Hmm. Sometimes I think that might not be a bad idea.

I used to laugh at this old bird. I used to think she was funny. My two years in Harlem have erased any amusement I might have found in her. Now I can see in how many ways she and women like her perpetuate a bad situation that is not getting any better. And it will get no better as long as she refuses to recognize and accept, as does my ex-friend, as I myself sometimes do when I am being stupid and cannot see, black reality for what it is.

The white woman in Cleveland, the ex-friend, the many many others who cannot see the limitations that exist, or refuse to believe them, refuse to believe *in* them, refuse to let them alter a sacred point of view: we have been, all of us, blinded by our resistance to other people's realities, perhaps even to reality itself.

Because I am not black, the white woman in Cleveland might have said, I cannot know black folks, cannot know what black folks know, nor can I feel what black folks must feel. Therefore I am lost.

Instead, refusing to put herself in someone else's shoes for a moment—and I mean as far into those shoes as she can squeeze herself—she can only see the result of the crime, the result of the shame, as when you walk down the street I live and see the burned-out car, the gutted abandoned buildings, the children pushed aside and ignored; she cannot see the shame itself. She cannot see that perhaps there is a reason behind it all. She cannot see that there is a difference between her life and the lives of her black neighbors. She cannot see that there is a difference between her life and Harlem. Nor can the woman who used to be my friend.

"I did it," she has often said—the same as I just said it. "Why can't those people?"

She had gotten pregnant when she was nineteen. She got married, she got divorced, she finished college, she found herself a decent job. Now she points a finger at herself.

"Why can't they do what I have done?" she argues. "Why don't they have enough initiative to break the cycle, to get off their rear ends and educate themselves, get good jobs, and take care of their children? Why can't the men stop selling drugs and stop shooting each other?"

I have asked her in reply, as calmly as I can, for I am prone to shrieking these days when white people start talking like white people: "What if they have no choice?"

"But there is always a choice!" she says.

You hear it all the time, from well-intentioned folk and from fools: "Those people have to take responsibility for what they do."

And she is right. At the same time she cannot see the safety net that was there to catch her when she fell: the fact that a man was there ready to marry her, that a job was waiting for him, that there was the support of two families— hers and his—in the wings just in case. And the biggest safety net of all: hope, based on the past. Without hope, there is nothing.

"I did it," she has said to me too many times. "Why can't they?"

She thinks she did it all on her own, and she cannot see how the hand of history has stacked the deck in her favor.

In 1675 Isaac Newton wrote to Robert Hooke a letter in which Newton said, "If I have seen further it is by standing on the shoulders of giants."

Newton could see that his achievements were built on the foundational work of the many thinkers who had preceded him.

If we, like Newton, can applaud this notion that beneath

the feet of every genius there are generations of thought upon which he stands, that there is a foundation of brick and wood and stone beneath every solid building, that behind every story of success there is a legion of forces that have made success possible, why can we not see just as clearly the pyramid of pain?

The white barber refusing to cut a black child's hair.

An old woman in Cleveland.

How many more of us see the isolated events of our lives as just that: isolated? We do not care to see, most of us, how the kind of disadvantage and atrophy that exist here in Harlem and wherever there is pain and problem do not just happen overnight. This kind of despair is generation upon generation in the making. The children born into it inherit more than a condition; they inherit a way of life, a way of living, a way of being. You can see the results of it every day in this neighborhood.

Most people outside the neighborhood do not care at all about this neighborhood nor about its sister-hoods. Even the ones who do care, do not care enough. Mostly we on the outside simply refuse any connection between this hood and our own, between these ills and ours. We refuse even to see the links in the chain, refuse to see the origins of this suffering, refuse to acknowledge our complicity in the perpetuation of it. We dodge the guilt we ought to feel and ignore the necessary steps that would help to end the suffering.

That's just the way it is, or the world wouldn't be the way it is.

What was done a long time ago has continuing and tremendous effect on the way things are today. What we do today and what we don't do today will take us a long way on the path toward heaven or hell.

Perhaps it takes a moment's reflection.

"Take away all of your kid's choices," I once said to the ex-friend. "All of them. Take away all possibilities and remove all hope. How do you think that kid will do?"

She replied without hesitation: "He'll do well in school, he'll work hard, he'll pull himself up."

She sounds an awful lot like that old white woman in Cleveland.

Though in truth I do not know what she sounds like, this woman with no name or address, I could hear her voice. Her voice was the voice that day of Antonio Morales.

"Yeah," Antonio was saying to me. "We are some bad men." And he said it with not just a little pride in his voice. I don't know if he intended it, but I think I also heard the mellowing edge of regret. "We do some bad things. Me, I've done a lot of evil shit but, man, I tell you, none of it as bad as what the people out there are doing to the people in here."

He was talking, quite naturally, about the people of Harlem, but when he spoke—and I don't know if he meant this either—he touched his chest, the way men do in Harlem, for emphasis, but he touched himself gently this time, without the heavy thump, and the way he looked when he spoke, I had the feeling that when he said "in here" he wasn't just talking about the physical confines of his neighborhood.

"But they just don't care," he said. "It's somebody else's problem. And the somebody elses of this world never seem to care."

And here again was that Pig Foot Mary twinge.

Try to imagine now, just for a second, how it felt at that moment to be who I am, how it felt to be as black as I am, as tall as I am, as broad as I am, a man who has seen a bit of the world now and who cowers in the face of very little, a man who can look nearly as fierce, when necessary, as anyone on these mean streets and who for all I know may even be as fierce as they are—nearly, perhaps, but not quite, for even as I was trying to project an image of manliness, of being streetwise and tough, of walking that walk that says *Don't fuck with me,* all the time there were tears in my eyes.

Try to imagine, then, how it felt wanting to show how strong you are, how unmoved by all of this you are. At the same time you want to cry. You want to put your arms around this guy, this man who has done so much evil, this Antonio Morales, because he is hurting, this man who has sold drugs to children, who has helped to ruin people's lives, who has possibly taken more than a few.

But then imagine his reaction if you did put your arms around him, if you said to him, "Man, somebody cares, Antonio; I care."

He would look at you and sneer, look at you and scoff, look at you and say, "Man, get the fuck away from me."

He would punch you hard in your chest with both fists at the same time—if he had two fists—and push you into the street, turn his back on you, and say, "Man, you crazy. Nobody cares about us. We don't count here, and you know it. You're just a fool." And he would never speak to you again.

Maybe I am a fool. Maybe Antonio would be right if he

said those things to me. Maybe nobody else does care—nobody but Wilson Clark and me—and that's not true, I know.

But I know too that Antonio is likely to be dead before too long.

Good riddance! the world will say, one less piece of scum floating on the cesspool of Harlem, one less worry for the rest of us. One less headache. One less human soul for anyone to care about.

God almighty! What are we saying? Antonio Morales used to be someone's son! His mother labored thirteen hours in the backseat of a Chevy so he could be born. She would have sold her soul for him, if she hadn't lost her soul already, given her life for him, if she had had much of a life to give. But so much already had been taken from her, she had little left. As the mother was denied, so too the son. As the mother gets discarded, so too her son. We just can't see it.

It's not just Antonio and his mother. It's Henry and Jolene. It's Nicky-No-Arms and *his* mother. It's the countless boys of countless women.

God, even Nicky-No-Arms was someone's son, someone who cuddled him in the cold and counted with him his fingers and his toes and never thought for a single second that on a particularly bad day some particularly bad men would take an axe and lop off his limbs and toss his arms and his fingers into a rubbish bin.

The boys doing the hacking that bad day, they too were someone's sons. Their fifteen-year-old pregnant girlfriends, these discarded mothers-to-be, they were someone's daughters. And the children who get discarded along with these young mothers: they are not just someone else's children but the young men's own, and the cycle never ends but goes on and on because this is what they have learned about life and love and caring for one another. This is what they have learned from us. This is what we teach them daily. The violence they know is the violence we taught them.

Yes! What they live and what they realize each day is what they have learned from the rest of us. Perhaps, then, discarded and uncared-for as they are, they are the sons and daughters of all of us, and this is how we have raised them.

I'm not trying to lay blame here . . .

(Like hell, I'm not. I just don't know where to put it. There are too many places where it fits the puzzle.)

But what if no one is to blame? Suppose what we see here in Harlem is nobody's fault. What then?

Perhaps it is all the result simply of the way we are somehow as a nation now, perhaps as human beings, and because there is no one to blame, there is therefore everyone to blame, just as it is everybody's problem—or soon will be.

Or maybe, as is too often heard, this is just the way things are. Maybe, as that look in Johnny Cannon's eyes suggested to me long ago, this is how it is and this is how it's supposed to be and this is how it will always be, truly and simply, and—I don't believe it, of course—there's nothing we can do about it, until . . . until . . . until it's too late.

No, I'm not trying to lay blame here. I think I'm smart enough to know that pointing a finger is the surest way to get a finger pointed back. Everybody has a thousand excuses for why things are the way things are. Everybody has a finger to point, and there are plenty of places to point it. When Pig Foot Mary is troubling me most, I even point the finger at myself.

I get the sense too that my father was pointing the finger at himself as well when he wondered if we had done things the right way, when he hinted at feeling somehow responsible. When he asked if I ever regretted the life I've lived, I wonder sometimes now if his question wasn't an accusation.

I stopped Antonio then, right there in the middle of the street as we crossed Malcolm X Boulevard. I didn't put my arms around him, though I wanted to, but I touched him on the shoulder just above the atrophied stump that used to be his right arm and I turned him toward me, purposefully, so he could see the tears in my eyes, and I said, "Somebody cares, Antonio. I care. That's why I'm here."

Something happens to those manly men on the streets when you corner them. Either they will enter with you into a confrontation and you will try to stare each other down, or they cannot meet your gaze and hold it. They will look everywhere but right back at you.

Antonio stiffened and shifted his regard from whatever was behind my left shoulder to whatever it was over my right. He looked up, he looked down, and only when I refused to let him look anywhere else did his eyes finally meet mine. I don't know if he meant what he said next or if he just said it so we could get out of the street and go on up to 114th and Malcolm X, but he said: "I know it, man. I know it."

But I don't know if he *really* knew it.

Either way, it made me feel better.

Then again, he never asked me, as if to say that caring is not enough, *But what are you going to do about it? What are you going to do with this life you're so happy with?*

A thousand times I have asked myself what it is I am doing here, wondering from time to time if this is some effort on my part to somehow save the world, and answering: God, I hope not.

It could be that I have been hoping only to save my own soul, and living in Harlem this short while has been no more than a feeble gesture.

Or it could be that I am simply trying to be Jan Karski, a Polish Catholic diplomat during World War II—not a Jew—who, when the world refused to believe the rumors about what the Nazis were doing to the Jews in Poland, had himself smuggled first into and out of the Warsaw ghetto, and then into and out of a Nazi concentration camp, so that his firsthand testimony might be listened to and believed where the same stories from Jews were taken as too self-serving to be heard and so for too long were ignored.

No. I don't really know why I am here. I only know this: Rather like Jan Karski, and unlike Nicky-No-Arms or Antonio Morales and now certainly unlike young Henry, I can always get smuggled back out again. Prisoner though I may be here, I can always leave.

It doesn't matter that I made a commitment to live here for one year that turned into two, no matter if I had come to stay for ten years or forever, still—and this changes everything—I can always leave.

Too many times I did leave, I suppose, to take trips—some long, some short—to get away from the city, to see something different, to experience something new. It is a luxury many Harlemites cannot afford, nor can one who wants to pretend to live the Harlem experience. Worries for my safety, worries that I might not fit in and therefore might never get beneath the surface of Harlem, these were the concerns others had about my coming here. For me, this ought to have been the biggest misgiving: that I might not do Harlem justice, might not spend as much time here as I should, for mine is a restless soul and I have not been known to stay in one place for very long. Since I was eighteen years old, my Harlem address has been my longest-kept address.

My friend Ann Plymouth chided me about this. She said I was too often gone from here, either out of town or simply away visiting friends who lived downtown and wouldn't come up.

"Being here part time is not enough," she said, and surely she was right, but no matter how many days and nights I spent here in a row, I could never know what they who live here know, nor truly feel what it is they feel.

I told Ann this, and she threw up her hands.

"Then why come here at all?" she shouted at me. "This

ain't no sideshow so you can go back waving your arms around and telling your downtown friends, 'I've seen it, I was there, yippee, and I survived.' We can suffer plenty without you pretending to be some great humanitarian from the Red Cross or something. This ain't no game for you to come up here and play at."

It wasn't funny, what she was saying, and of course she was right; we had had this conversation many times already. But when she is mad at me and shouting like that she has a way of making a fist with her tiny hand and holding it at her side as if she is waiting for me to do or say something stupid so she can smack me. And I always do. But she never does.

She has the smoothest skin, I think, I have ever seen. To hold her hand, caress her face, or to touch her arm is to know the physical equivalent of innocence. And when she smiles she can brighten any dark room or dismal situation. But when she is mad at me and her face is a scowl, she is at once a tantrum-throwing three-year-old and a weathered old woman you've cut in front of at the supermarket checkout, all wrinkles and fury and venom. The smoothness vanishes from her face, and she is rage.

I tried not to laugh. I couldn't help it, quickly moving to defend myself.

"It's not you," I said. "I'm not laughing at you. Honest, this time. It's just that you remind me of somebody." And I told her this story.

One night I took a bus home from downtown to Harlem. I had spent most of the afternoon and evening in Chelsea. I had cadged a meal from my friends Mat and Pam and had stayed late but didn't want to spend the night. In the early

189

midnight hours, I jumped onto the M-11 and rode the bus up to 133rd and Amsterdam.

The bus driver was a fellow named Gus. He is, or at least he was that night, one of those chatty drivers who, probably to avoid the boredom of routine, talks a lot into the PA system and announces each stop or each landmark as he approaches it. Jacob Javits Center. Forty-second Street. John Jay College. Lincoln Center. Seventy-second Street.

From Midtown into the eighties the crowd on the bus was a New York City crowd, black, white, Asian, Hispanic. But as the bus climbed into the nineties, the lighter colors got off. At Ninety-ninth Street, Gus made this droll announce-ment: "One Hundredth Street coming up next. Time for all you good white folks to jump off now and hurry on home."

He said it to be funny, but only slightly. The blacks and Hispanics who would ride the rest of the way to Harlem recognized the truth in what he was saying, nodded at one another, and laughed, but clearly there was irritation in Gus's voice. Gus is a black man.

Sure enough, one by one, street by street, the white folks did all get off. By 113th Street, blacks and Hispanics were the only ones left. But at 104th Street there were still four young white people on the bus, only four, the four of them friends. They had been talking and laughing the whole way up since 66th Street and making a lot of noise on the bus as if it were theirs, and now as three of them stood to get off they began making plans to get together again. When the bus stopped, two jumped off right away. The third lingered too long, saying good-bye to the fourth. Gus grew impatient and refused to wait. When the doors closed, Gus would not open them again and the bus pulled away.

"Hey, hey! Wait a minute. I want to get off." There was just the touch of panic in his voice, even though his friend was still on, probably a student at Columbia, and even though he would have only two blocks to wait and walk back.

Gus muttered loud enough for the folks in the front of the bus to hear.

"I got a schedule to keep," he said. "I can't be waiting for you to do all that hugging and kissing back there. This is the bus to Harlem. This ain't no ride at Disneyland."

The blacks and browns who were left laughed. And I laughed too, was laughing at Gus in fact when I laughed at Ann. She saw the connection but didn't think it was funny.

"Yeah," she said. "That's just the way it is, isn't it? Nobody wants to be here."

She glowered at me.

I knew she was not lumping me into a category with the white folks on that bus. Still, she had accused me many times before of playing at some game—or worse, of being like (in my estimation) Pig Foot Mary: here today, gone tomorrow, profit in my pocket.

I could have asked her what she would have me do instead, if I should turn my back forever on Harlem and not care at all, just go on about my business, but I already knew what she would say. I already knew what she wanted— without her ever having said it.

What she *had* said to me more than once was: "No. You

can't turn your back. You need to be here. I don't know what the reason is, but there *is* a reason for you to be here. You're supposed to be doing what you do, here today, somewhere else tomorrow, feeling life, feeling this particular life—for now. Maybe you're here to be a witness, to record all this stuff for some reason. I don't know."

She made me think suddenly of my father, who also, I have imagined lately, sees me, now that he takes my writing seriously, as the same sort of witness, someone who will tell what needs to be told, for nothing lives on merely because it once happened; lives vanish without a trace. It is the story-tellers who remember and tell their stories, the writers who re-create them and keep them alive. And the story of Harlem, like the story of my father, like so many other stories, needs to live on so that Harlem's children and our children and our children's children will one day know just how much was endured, and how much was overcome for their sake. Thus they may one day draw strength from the strength of those who went before them, and pride from pride, courage from courage.

For this reason, if for no other, I felt I needed to be here.

"But remember," Ann said, before she left me that day. "It's one thing to come here, another thing to really be here. You can't have the real thing just by living in Harlem a while and pretending to be poor."

It is true that in wanting to have the true black experience I had allowed myself to become poor. In somehow buying into the myth that life in an inner-city ghetto is the only *real* black experience, that you have to be poor and desperate to be truly black, that you have to be on welfare

192

to understand what goes on here in the black community, and in my feeble effort to really care, I have taken no jobs while I've lived in Harlem. In my effort to be like *them*, I earned no money. I spent every cent I had, then borrowed and spent some more. The pressure of living in debt increases for me daily. Even so, my experience can never be what *they* experience. I can always change the shoes I stand in, and instantly with them change my circumstance.

My father, in asking if I regretted the life I had so far lived, was wondering the same thing: What now? And what for?

For a long time after I moved into Harlem, I had no telephone. Again, it was an exercise in being poor. I don't know if Harlem is so different in this regard from the rest of Manhattan, from the rest of the country, but you need never travel far in search of a pay phone here. Very often the public phone on this corner or the next one, or the phone in front of the bodega up the street, inside the laundromat, or at the grocery store, very often these are not just instruments of convenience or of last resort. The pay phone here is primary. That's why there are so many of them. It seems cheaper to pay as you go, rather than shelling out a big sum once a month whether you use the phone one time or ten or two hundred. In New York City you pay for each call you make from your home. When you're very poor, the pay phone in the cold, in the rain, in the snow, probably seems a bargain.

I tried this for a long time in the beginning of my time in Harlem, having for my telephone only the public phones on the streets. It wasn't too bad at the start. At least I didn't have to run up and down the stairs each time I needed to use the thing. Whenever I had to make a call, I only had to look from my front-room window. I could see the phone down at the corner of 131st. I rarely had to wait in line. I could see if the phone was being used. I could not tell, however, if someone had ripped the handset away. It happened frequently. When that phone had been destroyed, there was always the grocery store half a block away on Amsterdam Avenue. It was a corner that was usually crowded. I often had to stand there and wait.

To what end all of this, I do not know. Trying to be like *them*, I suppose, trying still to know, still playing at being one thing or another until at last I tired of the inconvenience. It was the same as the living in Harlem: I could always leave, always change my circumstance. If I wanted a phone in my apartment, I could have one. Finally I did.

It was a combination of things that led me to get my own phone. I could never receive phone calls, for one thing. For another, the harshness of that first winter finally set in, and I decided I didn't very much like standing outside in the cold. If these reasons weren't enough, when night fell, of course, there were always the rats.

"Pop, Pop," I yelled once into the phone as I talked to my father about one thing or another. "Guess what, man, guess what. I just saw a rat as big as a Buick. It wasn't running, it wasn't even scampering. Man, it was just out for a Sunday stroll to the garbage and then back home."

"That's nothing," he said. "Brother, until you've seen a rat stand up on its hind legs, salute hello, and call you by name, you ain't seen nothing."

He didn't laugh. There was no giggle in his voice. He told it straight, as he did his best stories, telling me about a place he once shared with a family of rats.

"They used to call me Mr. Harris," he said. "But after a while I was seeing them so regular they started to get kind of familiar. They started calling me Sam."

Practically every time I used the phone after that, I spotted a rat or two or three. Nearby was the pickup point for someone's garbage. Just opposite, there was a chink in the stone wall. Rats went with ease and boldly from one to the other. I seemed to be the only person on the street even slightly unnerved. But the sight of rats will do that to me. Rats make me shudder.

I was walking home late one evening. If it was not quite the witching hour, it was certainly the hour of the rat. Convent Avenue that night was a rats' playground: rats on the trash cans, rats in the gutters, rats scurrying along the curbs.

At the corner of Convent and 128th, there is a vacant lot. A thousand rats must live there. The lot is overgrown with thick weeds that shuffle from time to time and rustle as if they are caught in a breeze. It is the movement of the rodents living there and stirring beneath the brush.

Out of the growth this night and onto the sidewalk strayed a baby rat. The adult rats in this neighborhood grow quickly into bold savages large enough to intimidate cats and small dogs—and me, of course. The baby rat was small enough that I continued on. I wanted to see where it would go, what it would do. I walked almost directly behind it. Directly behind me came the shrieking mother rat. She was large enough to scare me, and enraged that I seemed to be threatening the little one. She ran after me, nipped at my heels, and had me hopping and dancing a few seconds before I broke into a full sprint and ran to the end of the block. When I stopped to look back, the mother rat was still coming.

When I got clear, I stopped. I wanted to laugh. There was nothing so very funny about it.

"It's like I told you, man," said Eliot Winston when I told him about it. "We just get shit on."

On the day he said this, we were walking down Park Avenue, Eliot Winston and I, telling each other stories. I was telling him the rat story. He didn't find it amusing. He was telling me a horror story of his own, about his brother. He didn't find that story amusing either.

Suddenly he shouted.

"Just once, goddamn it! Just once I would like to know what it's like to be white in this country."

It is one of his favorite things to say when he is especially frustrated, but I wondered this time if maybe he hadn't meant to say "rich."

It was the morning rush hour and it was springtime, so the sky was still a little bit dark. The air was cool and crisp. Eliot took a deep breath. There were tears in his eyes, I thought from the bite of the cold air.

We had walked from 125th down into the nineties, and the landscape had changed completely. Tall buildings rose up all around us. Gone were the shabby storefronts with their barred windows, the four- and five-story tenement buildings, and the boarded-up shells in Harlem that nobody seems to own. Gone too were the vacant lots. The real estate in this neighborhood is too valuable to be wasted, to lie empty, or to be used for ugly housing projects. There are none here. Instead Park Avenue is lined on both sides with elegant high-rise apartment buildings that give way to the towering office buildings of Midtown. This is a part of town where beauty counts, where it matters how things look.

Eliot and I stopped there on the corner and looked in both directions, up Park Avenue toward Harlem, down Park Avenue toward the rest of the world. The railroad that runs aboveground in Harlem has gone underground by the time it reaches Ninetieth Street. The elevated tracks have gone from the center of the avenue. The rest of the way down to the forties, the center of the street is taken up by islands of grass and flowers. Park Avenue here has the look and feel of an urban paradise. It is a long way from Harlem.

Park Avenue that morning, as every morning, was crawling with cars that looked to me like some kind of molten lava spilled from the volcanic tops of these tall buildings, poured into the canyon floor below, and creeping slowly downtown. The lava glowed red taillights, white headlights, dimming as the day brightened, and yellow. Most of the cars were taxis. New York City, from this view in the middle of this street at this time of the morning, is a beautiful place. It is a different world from the world fifteen blocks away.

"Naw, man," Eliot said. "If I'd have meant rich, I would have said rich. I said white, and what I meant was white. Money ain't got nothing to do with it."

He had a look around and reassessed.

"Okay," he said. "Maybe money's got a little something to do with it."

I remembered then a story my brother Tommy had told me the previous summer.

My brother lives in the Connecticut suburbs of New York City. He is one of the millions who ride the trains into the city each day, who come in to their high-priced jobs and then go out again, who encounter places like Harlem usually only in passing, if at all. But on a hot Saturday afternoon my brother got a big dose of Harlem out in the suburbs where he lives.

It was the first summer after I moved to Harlem. Tommy and I had met, as we often did, for lunch at a Japanese restaurant near his office in Midtown. I was telling one story about rats, and another story about a man I had once seen shot (in New York City, but not in Harlem). I was complaining about how long it had taken for the ambulance to come. The one cop who finally did arrive stood around doing nothing but waiting like the rest of us. It was a story that came up because of a car accident I had recently seen in Harlem, where it always seems to take forever for an ambulance or for the police to come when you need them.

My brother, who is never glum, all of a sudden looked very grim.

He had been playing baseball the Saturday before, he told me, in a park in the leafy suburbs near his house. When his game was finished, he sat to watch another group of amateurs play. My brother loves baseball, he loves to play it, he loves to watch it, it doesn't matter if it's professional baseball or amateur baseball, big kids playing or little kids. He just loves baseball.

Somewhere on the field a man walking his dog had a heart attack and collapsed. The man was white.

Knowing my brother as I think I do, I would say he was probably more concerned about getting the game under way again than about the man clutching his chest. My brother checked his watch, he said. Someone else went and called an ambulance.

There is a look Tommy shares with my father, whom he resembles much more than I do. It is a look that holds seriousness but is edged with humor. It is a look that speaks of the kind of laughter that keeps you from crying, that keeps you from going too crazy.

"Someone had to go and call the ambulance," he said. "I mean, someone had to leave the field, find a phone, and make the call."

He told the story to be funny. He tells all of his stories to be funny. This time, though, he wasn't laughing.

"The ambulance came in about two minutes," he said. "Then another one came. And then two more. Finally a fire truck showed up." He laughed a little bit at the fire truck and then was all seriousness again.

"Two fucking minutes," he shouted. "Can you believe it?" He was shaking his head. "Man, it must be great to be white and living in America."

Eliot Winston was saying the same thing. He wasn't laughing either.

"They get the roast chicken," Eliot said. "We used to get some of the bones. Now we just get the chicken shit."

A black woman came round the corner where we stood. She was holding hands with two white children, walking them to school.

Another woman came hurrying up the street. She was being dragged by the seven dogs she was paid to take each day for their morning walk.

"Money's got something to do with it," Eliot said. "But it's more than that. Being white's got more to do with it, being white and not wanting anything to do with people who are black except to let them watch your children, clean your house, cook your dinner maybe, and walk your dog, that kind of shit. The whole problem is that white people are white, that's all it is. And white people think like white people. They just don't get it and, man! they just don't want to get it. And that's the real kick in the ass, let me tell you. It's a kick in the ass so hard you can't help but open your eyes wide. That's why in them old movies black people are always walking around with their eyes bugging out. It's 'cause they been kicked in the ass so hard and so often, their eyes just stayed like that."

He laughs a little bit, but only just a little.

"Just like when you were a kid and your mama told you not to cross your eyes 'cause if somebody slapped you upside the head your eyes would freeze that way. It's just like that."

The laughter stopped.

"Only now," he said, "we wear a different look. We don't be grinning all the time like we used to, we don't be having our eyes wide open and bugging out and putting the white folks at ease and making them laugh. Ain't no happy niggers no more. Everybody out here's mad. Now we be squinting all the time and frowning. Now we all the time tired 'cause we be working so goddamned hard and still ain't got nothing to show for it. I'm surprised every black man out here ain't killed somebody."

I thought just for a second then of Eliot's brother and the story Eliot had told me as we walked. But there wasn't time for reflection. Eliot filled all the empty spaces with his anger. He kept talking.

"And white people can't see a fucking thing," Eliot said. "We're tearing down the country, bleeding the place bankrupt with all this welfare shit, and teaching our children to surrender. And white people think they ain't got nothing to do with none of it but to keep the crime out of their neighborhoods—and keep the black folks out too, while you're at it; that's what they think the solution is for them, just put us aside and let us rot in the fucking filth they've stuck us in. Let me tell you one thing: as badass as we think we are, as powerful as we think we are, and might actually be, I don't know about that, but I know this: white people do not take us seriously. That's for damned sure. If they did, this shit would not be what it is."

The first time I saw Eliot Winston, he was saying pretty much the same thing. It was late one afternoon on the corner of 125th and Park Avenue, not far from where we now stood. There he was, that first time I saw him, beneath the elevated rails of the Metro North 125th Street station, where the trains carrying those commuters pause briefly to give them each a little thrill. This is as close as most of them will ever get to setting a foot in Harlem. From the tracks high above the streets, the commuters can get a pretty good look at Harlem's decay, Harlem's blight, a pretty good view of hell before the trains continue on their way to purgatory and paradise—to Grand Central Station and the rest of Manhattan in the one direction, and in the other direction either up the lush and peaceful Hudson River valley and the semirurality of quiet towns with names like Pleasantville; or on toward New Haven, Westport, Stamford, and all the little commutervilles in between. The little thrill these commuters get is akin to the jolt of adrenaline the au pair with the baby carriage got the instant she realized she was bound for Harlem: a moment's uncertainty, not knowing what could or what might or what will happen, just knowing that this is not the place to be; and the unacknowledged relief when the doors finally close and the train pulls away again, takes them away again, out of Harlem and gone.

They are not unlike the downtowners of old, those long-ago visitors who would come uptown to Harlem for a glimpse of Nigger Heaven and who would then be gone again. They had seen, they had been thrilled, they had survived. But they didn't want to—and were glad they didn't have to—stay here for long.

From time to time when I look from the front window of my apartment, a big tour bus will rumble by. It is almost funny to see the faces of the tourists pressed against the windows, their eyes wide to catch every juicy and exotic tidbit of this foreign land, their cameras ever ready. You see these same buses parked on 125th Street or on Malcolm X Boulevard in front of Sylvia's, where as part of their tour they can stop for an authentic Harlem meal in an authentic

Harlem restaurant. It is most noticeable on a Sunday, when the crowds of tourists make it often impossible to squeeze another soul into Sylvia's, when over on 125th Street the tourists and the vendors used to have the street nearly to themselves early in the day—that is, before the street vendors were exiled from 125th Street.

It is always good for a little laugh to watch the tourists venture gingerly from their buses, to watch them buy souvenir T-shirts from the vendors, to watch them snap photos of the Apollo Theatre across the street, to watch them walk from one corner to the next. But they never stray too far from the buses. It is as if they are tethered. They never let the buses out of their sight. When lunch is over or when the souvenir shopping is done, they all file back onto the buses, and they are gone once more, back whence they came, back to their own worlds far from this one.

And the vendors count the money they've made. They smile little smirks of victory. They mutter beneath their breath, and their eyes reveal it: be gone and good riddance to you!

And rightly so on the one hand. These visitors are the same lot who out West buy trinkets and blankets and beaded belts from the Indians at the trading posts that line the highways, or at the railway station in Gallup, New Mexico. They never notice that the curios they've bought were made in China. They think instead that they have tasted the culture, that they carry a bit of it home with them, even though they never even took their gloves off long enough to touch it, nor would they ever, and that is enough for them. It's on to the next stop on the tour. Indians back to the reservation. Harlemites back where you belong. Back to the margins, all of you, out of sight and out of mind and off the pages completely.

Good riddance, then, to them and theirs. So say the visitors on leaving, whether they know it or care to admit it. So say too the ones who are left behind. *Good riddance!* It becomes their battle cry.

"Christ, man!" Eliot once shouted at me. "We say that shit and we believe that shit and we live that shit every day. And every day we think we're winning some goddamned victory. But every day we're losing one. We're so goddamned stupid we don't even know it. They win, we lose, and we cheer about it. What could be stupider than that, or better for white folks? They get what they want, and we get nothing—less than nothing, when you sit and think about it—and we think we've hit the jackpot."

Eliot tends to rant when he talks about being trapped.

"God! Just once," he shouted. "Just for a little while, I just want to know what it's like to be white in this country, just so I could look at black people and laugh at us like white people must be doing."

When I saw Eliot the first time, there outside the Metro North station, he was ranting at someone else. The man who that time was the object of Eliot's attention stood rather passively, almost unconcerned as Eliot beat the air with his long arms and vented his spleen. The man seemed to have heard Eliot's tirades before and was used to them. He paid as much attention to the passing cars, to the buses, and to the people going into and out of the station as he did to anything Eliot was saying. This man, I found out later, was Eliot's brother, T. C. Abernathy—same mother, different fathers—and as I passed he glanced at me from under one of Eliot's outstretched arms. He smiled briefly as if to reassure me. Eliot saw the smile somehow and the glance and turned to watch me go slowly by.

It was the start of a long moment that took place in slow motion. I am a slow walker anyway, can be very slow indeed, and this day, as I was not in a hurry yet, I was taking my time and strolled most casually in front of Eliot and his brother. Eliot's eyes and mine met and locked in a stare that goes beyond interest but seems rather some kind of primitive challenge mutually issued, mutually accepted. I walked past. Eliot followed me with his eyes. He finished what he was saying to T.C., and although it was part of the long lecture already going on and had nothing to do with me, it stabbed my ears as if it had been directed at me.

T.C.'s gaze shifted in this long slow moment from Eliot to me and back again twice before I reached the corner. We all three sensed something. Probably none of us knew exactly what.

Slowly, Eliot's flailing arms came down to his side. One hand rested on a hip. His body was still turned toward his brother, but he had turned head and neck and was looking in my direction. I had stopped at the corner and stood there waiting. The long moment continued.

The light was green, and I could have crossed. I waited until it turned red. Then I turned completely around and looked back.

T.C. had folded his arms across his chest and had stepped back to lean against the chain link fence behind him. He was out of the arena now.

On the fence the two brothers had hung the T-shirts that they were selling. Printed on these shirts were photos of Malcolm X, and beneath the photos were slogans. There were other T-shirts besides, and other things for sale, but only the Malcolm X shirts were on hangers and hung on the fence. When T.C. stepped back out of the line of eyesight fire, he tipped one of the hangers and one of the T-shirts fell. The long moment was broken. Eliot turned then to yell at his brother. And I was free to continue on my way to work, across 125th to Lexington Avenue and down to 103rd, over to Third Avenue and through the housing projects to Second Avenue, past the drug dealers who crowd the corner there and the first half of the block, and down the street to Exodus House, where I had become a teacher in an after-school program.

But I wasn't free yet, not really. Anyway, I didn't continue on. I couldn't. Not right away. I had to wait a little longer. The slow-motion moment had ended, but now I had moved into one where time stood utterly still.

It was one of those moments that brings everything into sharp focus, a moment through which one views clearly everything one has ever seen and everything one has ever done. It was one of those moments like all moments—though we hardly seem to notice it—that looks backward in time and forward in time all at the same time, and I could see at once all that I had seen in Harlem and all that I had done and all I was about to do. It was a moment through which I could examine everything I had yet done in my life and everything I would ever do. It was a moment that called into question everything there is about what it means (to me) to be black and what it means, in fact, to be me, an instance of such clarity that I could not miss the significance of the moment nor could I ignore it, and I could see right the way back to the barber refusing to cut my hair, back to Johnny Cannon doing his stabbing, back beyond even that, back to all the moments that connected then and now. I could see as well, so I tell myself now, into the not very distant future, though I hardly knew it at the time, and if I couldn't really see into the future, I could certainly feel my way forward at least as far as that late night and early morning when I would look out my bedroom window and knew I had to do something, knew too that I *would* do something.

Little by little the curtain parts. Little by little light splinters the darkness. Suddenly I saw what I had come to Harlem to see.

Standing on that corner that day, I could see it all and hear it all and my ears burned from what Eliot had said as I passed, his arms flying out, his hands coming back to his chest, and then that final gesture that seemed to suggest surrender: arms out, hands open and empty, palms up.

My ears burned as if Eliot's words were igniting the dry kindling of all I had heard in Harlem, and the smoke from the fire in my head filled my eyes, and what I could see, I saw through a veil of shimmering haze. What I saw and what I heard were the sounds and images of surrender.

Harlem is not all surrender, of course, the same as it is

not all tired and lifeless misery. All is not the cliché of poverty that we've come to expect here, but the cliché overrides all else. Its images are powerful, and its reality is the one that matters here, for here and everywhere else life is defined not from the top down, as some might have you believe, but upward from the bottom where the numbers are greater. Notwithstanding the elegant homes that survive in Harlem, notwithstanding those who continue to strive, the doctors the lawyers the businessers and the woman over whose shoulder I peeped at the cash machine where I spied the surprising amount of money in her checking account—and who knows how much other money hides in Harlem—despite all this, when you stand on a street corner in Harlem and you see what Harlem has been saddled with, what Harlem has become from what Harlem once was, what Harlem has settled for and what Harlem continues to settle for, it is easy to see the ground beneath the things that Eliot was saying. It is easy to see the trap into which I and so many others had fallen.

"The black man is finished," he said. "We are lost, man, and we don't even know it—so how can we ever find our way? We're through."

These are the words that started the fire that singed my lobes, that filled my eyes with smoke. These are the words that froze my footsteps, that locked me in place.

I was wearing white silk trousers that day and a lavender shirt. I looked decidedly out of place, and easy it would have been for me to imagine that Eliot's words had been generated by the sight of me and directed at me in ridicule. Not many weeks before, I had been similarly reprimanded by a street vendor for walking down 125th Street with a woman at my side. The woman was white. I cannot remember if we were even talking, she and I, but certainly we were not holding hands, and there was nothing in our manner to suggest that we were anything more than two people sharing the same sidewalk. "Don't forget your race, man. Don't forget your race." He was pointing at me as I passed.

Eliot was not pointing, but he did follow me with his gaze, and easy it would have been for me to take offense, feel a threat, respond in kind. I could have walked over calmly to him and demanded to know if he was referring to me. That would have been enough to get the show started. That would have been the easy way.

It may have been fear that kept me from puffing out my chest and challenging Eliot. It was a warm day. He was wearing a tight T-shirt that showed how muscular and strong he was. His brother was even more so. Although T.C. had smiled as I went by and seemed to take himself out of this showdown between Eliot and me, with men on the street, especially with brothers, you never know when a dispute is going to become a two-against-one situation. It may have been fear that kept me from moving, but I don't think so; it seems I am a confrontational sort.

Very late one night I was riding the subway home to Harlem from somewhere downtown. It was the hour when the trains are mostly empty and the subway can be a bit unsafe, left to those who have little choice but to ride the subway late in the night, those who work the awkward shifts, those who have no place else to sleep. The only others you find at that hour are those few who think nothing of the potential danger, the brave and the naive, and those looking for trouble. On this night six of the ones looking for trouble got on the train at Fifty-ninth Street and immediately began harassing the brave and the naive.

The brave are never so brave as to confront. They look away and hope only that they will be left alone. You could almost hear sighs of relief when the six thugs spotted a naive young girl alone and zoomed en masse to hover over her. Those at the other end of the car looked away.

The young girl sat across the aisle from me. One of the six sat on the seat beside her. Another stood near them. Two others stood by the door. The last sat directly opposite me. He was the youngest of them. He had the most to prove. The two with the girl teased her. They started talking to her and asked her name and for a long while she ignored them. When they asked for a cigarette she broke down and reached into her purse and took out a pack. When she opened the purse one of the young boys reached in and made a grab for her wallet, but he got nothing, laughed, and said he was only kidding. Now the one who had stood sat beside her too and they talked. I watched it all, said nothing, just witnessed.

The young boy opposite me watched me. He too said nothing. Then I turned to watch him watching me, and we stared each other down. It's what men do. He wanted me to look away. I defied him, I challenged him, I stuck my feet out in the aisle, crossed my arms and continued to look at him.

All of a sudden the boys teasing the girl stopped. Their

attention now was on us, the starers. The two by the door watched us as well. The boy across from me finally got up and stood right in front of me.

"What you looking at, man? You looking at me?"

I said nothing. I only nodded. Slowly.

"What's your problem? Why you staring at me?"

One of the two by the door came and sat to my right. He seemed the oldest. He seemed the leader of this band. He leaned forward, elbows on knees.

"What's the problem?" he said. "Why you staring at him?"

There was one on my left by the door, this young boy standing inches away in front of me, my eyes locked on him, and there was one sitting beside me.

It would have been easy to capitulate. Too easy. It would have been very easy also to do the expected in such a situation, to leap to my feet, grab the little one by his throat and shake him dead like a terrier killing a rat, and then try to take out one or two of the others before they killed me, or fight them off until the train stopped at 125th and the doors opened and I could flee. And then what? What happens to the girl once I angered these boys? What happens to her anyway?

These scenarios and considerations were among the thousand thoughts I scanned as I waited for the next gambit. But all the choices were the easy ones, the too easy ones. Perhaps there was a better way, a way untried, a way we could all win.

The ringleader beside me gave me this chance.

"What's the matter, man, you having a bad day?"

"Just like you, man," I said to him. "Every day's a bad day."

It was as if he had been lightly jabbed. His head snapped back just a little. A *hmmph* tried to escape but got trapped in the back of his throat. He nodded. He smiled. Then he laughed. They all started laughing. The young one in front of me was the last to catch on, but he laughed too. He laughed because the others laughed. And the tension cleared.

When the train stopped at 125th, they all got out. I waited until just before the doors closed, then I got out too. The girl stayed on. I don't know now which path was easier, didn't know then.

Stuck on a street corner in Harlem, unable to move, I still didn't know which path was easier.

The turnabout was slow, and the walk was long back to where Eliot stood waiting for me. His hands were on his hips now. He was definitely waiting. And I was suddenly but just as definitely angered—but at whom; at what?

I turned. I looked at him. I felt the hot flush of my outrage. Not so much at what he had said. Not so much at the way he watched me and seemed to challenge me. But at everything. And it hit me all at once.

"The black man is finished," Eliot had said. *"The black man is through."* And I wished to God in that moment that somehow Eliot had been right. I looked up and down all the streets and avenues that fed into the spot where we now stood, and I could see clearly—if I hadn't known it already before—that unfortunately Eliot was dead wrong. The black man was not dead. Not yet.

Harlem had been born and Harlem had slipped toward death too quickly, seems often and in many ways to have been almost stillborn, as if it never had a chance to achieve very much of the fullness or the richness of life beyond its first glorious breaths, withering then and nearly dying, and yielding, as the fruit of its flowering, the black man who as black man, like the night-blooming moonflower, ought similarly to have flourished brilliantly and dramatically, which the black man did, and ought then to have died suddenly and vanished away, which he did not. The black man was never allowed to die.

And in dying, to come to life again and live.

But though the end of Harlem came in a way swiftly, the end of the black man about which Eliot speaks is and has been for a long time the lingering death of decay, the burning and smothering death of a garden that has been buried in an acid fertilizer.

The turnabout was a slow one, and it took us away from all the hope and possibility that Harlem of old had once generated. At the same time it was perhaps much too quick, should not have happened this way at all, I don't suppose, but it was as inevitable, given the tenders of the garden, as my turning around, given the man that I am, to confront Eliot head-on. And now I don't know if I am to celebrate the dying as part of some new beginning, if indeed there is a new beginning, or mourn, but on this corner as I look all around and up and down the avenues and streets that feed into this place, into this moment, I feel cheated that Harlem is not what Harlem was. I feel cheated and angry that I must continue to live as a black man who ought to have died by now, whom Eliot thinks *has* died.

On this corner I feel shamed that I have allowed myself to fall into this trap that I—and many of us here—even now embrace.

On this corner I feel at the same time absurdly guilty about having left Harlem—*absurdly* because, if my argument is to make sense, then I ought to be glad those who got out of Harlem did indeed get out, like Pig Foot Mary, who springboarded from here and into the wider world and refused, inasmuch as was possible in her time, to settle here, refused to be content with what she would have had to settle for here.

Yet I cannot help but wonder, as my father wonders, if in springboarding away from Harlem we who did leave are not somehow responsible for the condition of Harlem and those who have been left behind, and wondering if, had we remained, Harlem might have been somehow different. Always that question. As if Harlem needed us and still needs us in some way.

We have these two histories, it seems—these two histories at least: the one we've lived and continue to live, and the other stories we might have known if we had made better choices, or worse ones, but anyhow different ones. We are stuck now certainly with the one, for good or for bad, and we're left to look at the others and can only wonder what has happened to us, what we've done to and for ourselves. We are left to wonder why, of course, and left to wonder what might have been, but we cannot change the past; we can only wrestle with the future.

The past hangs over us like a mighty promise made and never kept, and I cannot escape—not only the questions and the wonderings, but the very notion that we (here again the ego speaks, and speaks loudly) who maybe should have stayed in Harlem didn't. We left. And Harlem was left to die.

As fine a vision as it may be to see beauty rising from decay, to watch the butterfly emerging from its cocoon, we ought to remember as well that as we float to the heavens to dry the dust on our wings, we have left behind the many others struggling still in the cocoon. We ought to remember that perhaps there is a collective cocoon and that we should all worry about it. It is the reason for the silk trousers, I think, and the purple shirt.

It was all there, then, at once and suddenly, the whole of it, on this corner and in these moments: the trousers and the shirt, the rats and the telephone and the taxis, the waste and the settling and the whole of Harlem, this magical place whose importance very well might reach far beyond the physical, as perhaps it might always have done, and into the realm of something much more soulful and sorrowful, something even spiritual.

I wondered then if this was what Herbert Washington had refused to explain and wanted me to discover.

I had come to Harlem and had pretended to be someone else. It was this that Ann Plymouth had warned me against, this coming to Harlem and pretending to be poor, allowing myself in fact to *be* poor and thinking that by doing this I could more easily seem one of them, as if to be truly black I had to be poor, had to use the pay phone down the street from my apartment, had to walk a certain way, talk a certain way, dress a certain way, and not mind the rats, the roaches, and the mice, that I had to be one thing or another and settle for less, that I had to imprison myself body mind and spirit.

I heard of a writer who came to Harlem once and felt

conspicuously out of place and endangered. He bought clothes to make him look like a ghetto child. He went to a barber and asked for a haircut that would help him fit in. He wrote a very standard story. He had accepted the standards that are set for Harlem, and he believed in them—for those around him and for himself while he was here. He tried to camouflage himself.

I once thought like him, thought that to be safe here, to be accepted here, and to have anyone to talk to here, I had to pretend to be someone else. I think now it is the wrong way to think.

Without meaning to, I had fallen far enough already into the trap that imprisons us all: an insular life. We allow ourselves to be cut off from the rest of the world by race and class; we even encourage the segregation and the pitiful, usually thoughtless, acceptance of the way things are that such isolation leads to. In the process we limit ourselves even as we attempt to limit and control others, to narrowly define them and decide who is, what is, and who can be. Into this trap we fall so willingly. If I could help it, I would fall in no farther.

Along the West Side of Manhattan runs the Seventh Avenue/Broadway subway line. The 1 train and the 9 train make the local stops, the 2 and the 3 are the express trains. At 96th Street the two express trains branch off to the east and cut across Manhattan beneath the northern tip of Central Park. The 3 train goes farther uptown; the 2 goes over into the Bronx. If you want to go farther up along the far West Side, unless you're already on the local train, you must get out at 96th Street and from there take the 1 or the 9.

They both continue up Broadway, and the next stop after 96th Street is the Cathedral Parkway stop. It is also called 110th Street. The subway conductor will announce it for you.

But even if you make the change, the next stop goes by the same name—110/Cathedral Parkway. It is not at all the same stop.

The 1 and the 9 trains stop at the 110th Street station, which is on the corner of Broadway, right at the doorstep of Columbia University. The 2 train and the 3 train stop at 110th and Lenox.

If you are on your way from Midtown or downtown to, say, Columbia, and you've taken the 2 or the 3 and you happen to be gabbing with your friends or napping or reading the paper or in some other way not paying close enough attention, you might easily forget to make the change. Surprise! You could find yourself coming up from the subway in a part of Harlem that you were not expecting.

Camellia Scott grew up not far from the Harlem station where the 2 and the 3 trains stop. She remembers how she and her friends would wait around at the top of the steps and how they would laugh when people came up bewildered and quite shocked to be in a neighborhood they did not recognize.

"You could tell they had made the big mistake," she told me. She spread her hands wide apart in front of her when she said it: *The big mistake!*

"You could see it in their eyes, that panicky look. It was funny to watch the way they stood in one spot and turned all the way around. They could never figure out what they were doing there alongside the park. And by the panic in their faces you could see them asking themselves why there were so many black people all around—black folks everywhere, and they all seemed to be staring. That's how it is when you feel out of place, and they weren't used to it; you could tell: all those black folks staring at them and laughing? And they were just as confused as could be, those white people coming up out of the subway. They were always white people, completely lost, out of their element and afraid, and it was nice for a change to have white people trapped in a world that was not theirs. This one was ours. And boy! did we laugh at them and throw things and just terrorize the hell out of them. We wanted them to know that this place was ours, and that here *we* had all the power."

That was when Camellia was a young teenager. She doesn't live in Harlem anymore. She had to move away, she said, because eventually she fell victim to the same trap she had once laid for the white folks. She went off to college. She got a job at a big bank downtown, where she analyzes overseas currency markets and evaluates the risk of foreign currency speculation. She makes good money. She wears nice clothes to work. She stays very late sometimes at the office.

"After a while," she said, "it got so that I was afraid to go home after work. People would be sitting out on the stoops and hanging out at the corners and they would say mean things to me and about me as I passed. Even if they said nothing, there was something in their eyes that spoke of threats. I didn't belong there anymore. Harlem wasn't mine anymore. I was an outsider. So I moved away. I went downtown."

Who could blame her for being afraid, for feeling excluded, for feeling that Harlem belonged to others and that she now ought to stay away and cannot go there?

If the answer is No one, then how can you blame the yellow taxi drivers who, except on rarest occasions, will refuse to come this far uptown? You hardly ever see yellow cabs on the streets of Harlem. They just don't come up this far. As a consequence many black fares are left standing on downtown avenues. Many cabbies will assume that black fares heading uptown are going home to Harlem and too often will refuse to pick them up.

The drivers themselves will tell you, Yes, that it's the law, that they have to drive you there—to Harlem or anywhere else in the city—if that's where you want to go. In practice it is quite another thing.

A driver downtown said to me, "Sorry, buddy. I just don't go up there."

He knew, of course, about the taxi commission's rule.

"Look, bud," he said. "I know all that stuff. It's like the law, or something. And I know what you probably are thinking. But I don't drive into Brooklyn either, and it's not just some racial thing. It's just too hard to get a fare coming back into the city, so I got to come back empty. And if I'm driving around empty, I'm not making any money."

"And that's the only reason?" I asked. "That's all there is?"

"Yeah," he said. "That's all it is." But I saw his eyes in

the rearview mirror, and they were watching me watching him. "It's just too far away," he said slowly—very slowly— then added, "And it's too fucking dangerous."

And who can blame him? Forty-one taxi drivers had been killed in New York City that year, most of them in the Bronx and in Harlem. Who can blame cab drivers for not wanting to go there?

Who can blame Camellia Scott or Pig Foot Mary or Joseph Carver, who felt unsafe, who left Harlem, who moved to Brooklyn? Who can blame the white folks who don't come up, who don't live here, who don't want to be here? Who can blame Camellia Scott and her young friends for their gloating response: Go away from here, we don't want you here, this is ours?

Who can blame them all for falling into a trap that has been camouflaged for so long and that they cannot see?

Go away from here, this is ours, we don't want you here.

(And the counterpointing voices: *Yes indeed, this is theirs.*)

How the voices sting in my ears, the times I've seen these words in action, the times I've said them myself!

And this is what those words, those actions, the sentiment, have brought us to. Here is where we stand.

A white woman I knew walked along 125th one evening in the direction of the subway station at St. Nicholas Avenue. It was raining. It was getting dark. Three men blocked her path, she told me, and made her change direction. She crossed the street, they crossed with her, in front of her, and when they got close enough to her, they muttered at her: "Uh-uh, bitch. Not here." And that was all. They wanted nothing else but to scare her and let her know where she did not belong.

A white man I knew worked for a time at the Paul Robeson Health Center on 125th Street. He left work one afternoon, walked to the bus stop on his way home. He was attacked on the street and beaten. The men who jumped him did not take his wallet. They did not demand money. They only wanted him to know where he was and whose neighborhood it was.

Whose neighborhood is this, whose world?

I remember the walk I took when I first moved to Harlem. It was a rainy day, but warm, and I wore no coat. I had found my apartment and moved in and now was feeling out the blocks that would be my new neighborhood. I felt truly at home in Harlem, happy to be black, happy to be in a black place. I turned the corner from Convent Avenue onto 145th Street, and in the doorway of the church that is there, two Asian men huddled beneath the portico to keep out of the rain. They could have been Korean shopkeepers who lived in the neighborhood, could have been Japanese tourists. I saw them from across the street and all I could think was, *What are you doing here? Go home, get away from here. Get on the bus and go. This does not belong to you, this is ours.*

And there it was. I had fallen into the trap that divides this country into at least two worlds, the one world black and the other world white, with the barriers that separate them rising like mountains, the one world so willingly trying to isolate itself from the other.

Hundred Twenty-fifth Street, now and for a long time the

main street of Harlem, was once the shopping center for the white folks, mostly Irish, who lived on the West Side above 116th. It was a time of separation. Blacks were not welcome to shop on 125th Street, even after Harlem had become the black quarter of New York City. Nor, for the most part, were they even allowed to work in those stores, not even to serve the white people who shopped there. The separation of these two worlds, black and white, was nearly total, and almost entirely at the discretion and whim of the world that is white.

Now again we find ourselves in an era of separation. Except for the tourists on Sunday, and here and there the odd white soul brave enough to venture up to Harlem, the one world and the other world are not a part of the same world. At any rate, they do not intersect anywhere near Harlem, for Harlem sits on the edge of a shelf far away from the centers of power and privilege, and to be here is to be acutely aware of this isolation, I would think. To be here is to be waiting always to be swept off the table altogether, onto the floor and into some corner where we go seemingly choiceless but at the same time all too freely.

On the corner of 125th and Amsterdam sits a huge housing project named for General Grant. It is tall and massive and made of yellowish brick. It takes up two of the four corners and spills down Amsterdam for another block or so.

On many occasions I have stood on that corner and tried to count the people who live there—not one by one, of course, but counted the windows, counted the numbers of floors, guessed at how many apartments there might be on each floor, and multiplied by a reasonable four people per apartment. By my crude calculations there must be over thirty thousand people living in this housing project—if you can call it living. Certainly those who dwell here consider it living. It is home to them. It has become what they know. But there are more people living on this corner than in the whole of the suburban hometown where I grew up.

Lashae Anthony lives in a housing project just like this one, but on the east side of Harlem. It is the only world he knows, the only home he has. He says he likes living there because his housing project is better than the other projects: cleaner, safer, nicer.

In what way nicer? "Just nicer," he would say, in that shy way he had then. He was only thirteen years old at the time.

It was, of course, and certainly to the untrained eye, no better, no worse, than any of the other housing projects, but it was where he lived. It was his. It was home. And he had only one project against another upon which to base his comparison.

It is amazing the things we can get used to when we force ourselves. It is perhaps still more amazing what we get used to if we allow ourselves even a moment's complacency. And quite simply it astounds me the things we will settle for and take comfort in once we convince ourselves, This is ours! No matter what the *this* is.

In the blood rush of recent memory, in the four seconds before I walked over and stood face to face with Eliot, the mind races and I cannot disregard the conflict that stirs within.

On the one hand I can understand the impulse for separation.

On the other hand I see it as little more than surrender, little more than the kind of blind acquiescence that Eliot once spoke to me about, a kind of self-inflicted isolation that plays right into the applauding hands of those who seek the separation and who profit somehow from it.

It is to me surrender, but of course I see the world from a particularly advantaged vantage point and think, rightly or wrongly, that there is nothing I cannot have, do, or be.

Similarly, there is in San Diego a woman of European complexion who struggles with this same question. She is in law school there, and she joined the Black Law Students' Association. She was told she was not welcome there, that she did not belong.

Likewise, a university professor who is white is repeatedly given a similar message. She teaches black studies, she teaches the writings of black authors. It was not easy for her to find a job. Oftentimes students and faculty have resented her presence. The same sentiment is at work here: This area is not hers; she does not belong here.

If this is true, if the one can't be part of a black studies program and the other can't join a group of black students, how in theory can a complaint be raised against black exclusion from the country club, from the halls of power, from the chambers of the boards of directors, from inclusion in general? If we crave this separation and are happy with it, where then the grievance, and why then the desire to share in what some will say is not ours?

Yes yes yes! I can already hear the argument that there is a difference. And perhaps there is, the difference having to do with a history of exclusion, a history of being oppressed, a history of all the time knocking on doors and never being allowed to enter, and *now finally we have something that is ours, and we want to keep it for ourselves and for us alone:* a place where we can let our hair down and for once not have to deal with white people, a place where we can go and be on our own, prosper on our own, celebrate ourselves, define ourselves, and meet our own needs.

Perhaps, then, there is a value in the ghetto—not only in this ghetto, but in ghettos of every kind: places where people of like mind and similar experience, people who look alike and think alike and share the same ideals and goals, the same ideas, the same dreams, desires, and ambitions and the same culture, can come together and live in peace away from all the others—whoever the others might be.

Perhaps there is value indeed in living in a ghetto, but the arguments we use to ghettoize ourselves are the same arguments the others use when they wish to exclude us and keep the treasures for themselves. Just as Eliot does, I wonder who ultimately comes out the big winner.

All I have to do is remember the walks I have taken. There is life on these streets, there are children playing, people laughing, lovers courting, and ball players shooting hoops on the playgrounds. There is music that streams from the apartments on the route from my apartment to Riverbank Park where I sometimes go to hit tennis balls, and music that booms from cars parked on 135th, music pouring from the shops on East 116th. But amid the life and the music, there are people standing around with nothing to do and nowhere to go, too much trash on every street, houses boarded up, buildings burned out, and housing project after housing project, named for someone named Grant, named Carver, named Robinson, named Lincoln, named for famous blacks or for people in history who were sympathetic to the black cause.

I looked at Eliot, I looked up and down the nearby streets, I waited to see what the next step might be.

I recalled in those few moments of stillness my first days in Harlem, those heady, electrifying days when I could feel Harlem's history upon my shoulders and the burden seemed such an easy one to bear, when I was more than happy to be trapped here in the ghetto, when I was in fact thrilled to be here, here in what once was the center of the black universe, here where in former times had come the many others who dreamed of creating the kind of haven that would serve as shelter where black folk could celebrate themselves, define themselves, cultivate themselves before they sprang forth into the wider world.

And so they came to Harlem—many in body, many in spirit only—from out of the South and from all corners of the black world: the businessmen, the educated, the politicians, and the skilled workers—to live in this ghetto that they might not have to live in some other ghetto.

And they came sowing the seeds of disaster, for it can be said that they who migrated north from the Deep South abandoned in many ways those blacks who remained there and left them bereft of shining example, left them too, it can be argued, bereft of leadership.

They came as well the slackers and the vagabonds and the ruffians, the unskilled, the under- and the uneducated who were left behind with the simply unlucky and once again found themselves bereft of shining example, bereft of leadership when they flew away, those who could fly from here. Pig Foot Mary. My father. I, myself.

Those who remain can claim pride of ownership, yes, can settle in and be content with what they have and can keep others out. But what they fight so hard to maintain as their own seem so often and in so many ways leftovers at best, and more often the sweepings of the street piled high off to the side or in some corner, discarded crumbs and refuse that really aren't *ours* but rather the giveaways, the throwaways, what has been picked over and what remains— not ours because we don't lay claim to it until it is already given to us.

"That," Eliot said, "is what I mean when I say the black man is finished."

I had turned around, and I had thought long enough now about which was the right move to make. I knew, of course, which would have been the easy thing to do, but easier is not always right, not always better.

Many were the nights during my time in Harlem that I came up from the subway at St. Nicholas and 125th and walked the rest of the way home. Many were the nights that I walked to Sylvia's to get a bite to eat, or went over to La Famille on Fifth Avenue to listen to music, or sometimes even I was just out for a stroll. When the weather was warm enough—and it didn't really have to be so very warm, just not so frigid—somewhere along the way of my walking I always came across men bunched together in groups on one street corner or another.

I don't know what any others think or feel when they encounter these same groups of men blocking the sidewalk, but always inside me buzzed a little electric tingle of apprehension, almost fear, and always always there was the thought that I should go around them, cross the street maybe, find another route to take. Always always I chose to walk straight toward them. If they were blocking the sidewalk, I would walk right into the middle of the pack and part them, touch one of them on the shoulder or on the back, and say "Excuse me, fellows."

It seems such a simple thing to do, perhaps not an easy thing, but a simple one. And you can see what it says: that I'm not afraid; or that if I am afraid, I'll not show it, I'll not act like it. But it says one thing more, and this one thing may be the truly important part: that those men on the corner, those men standing in a crowd on the corner—they are not to be deferred to, they are not to be treated as if they are to be avoided and feared and kept at a distance. In other words, I would not let them change my path, my thinking, or my way of being. I would not, in fact, let them change me, for to change would be all too easy.

If I were to act any other way, then like that other writer visiting Harlem I might as well buy the clothes that would make me fit in here, try to camouflage myself, walk the way a ghetto child is supposed to walk, talk the way a ghetto child is supposed to talk, and buy into the image as projected, the image as perceived and accepted. Then once more I would be wearing that look of surrender that confesses how much I believe what I have been told about them—and about myself.

I choose therefore not to believe all that I have been told. I prefer to see for myself. My father long ago had given me that choice. It lay in his mandate that I create for myself a world of my own, one that not only would make sense for me but that I could put my faith in. And I simply cannot believe in a world that seeks to diminish me or to erase me completely. So I preferred not to alter my walk, my talk, the way I look, or the paths I take.

Of course there was that one time not so long ago when I was left questioning the wisdom of my beliefs, my certainty, and my stubbornness.

I had taken an afternoon stroll and was walking along 149th Street, between Broadway and Amsterdam. A young man was talking to his girlfriend. He had that look of romantic bravado about him, and he took up more space on the sidewalk than he needed or had a right to.

She sat on the short stack of steps in front of her building. He sat on a box a little left of center along the path. Behind him, in one of those shallow wells that passes for a planter, a skinny tree tried to grow. The girlfriend was leaning back, resting on her elbows and arms, her legs stuck out straight, crossed at the ankles. The young man leaned forward over a tiny table where they had placed the two cans of soda they were drinking. They took up practically the entire sidewalk. Two other young men and a young woman stood nearby.

The boy looked up at me as I approached and then turned away nonchalantly. Without a word, he was speaking to me and telling me how this was to be played out; clearly I was supposed to go around them both. He didn't care that I would have to step either off the sidewalk and into the street or into the muddy little well. His only worry was that I not disturb him.

I wonder what I might have done had he been older, bigger, and looked stronger. I wonder what he might have done if the girl and a couple of his pals had not been there and he had been alone.

I knew what I was supposed to do and I did it. I stepped past this young boy and his young girl, stepped over her outstretched legs and tipped the little table with my knee. I excused myself as I passed through, held my hands out in a gesture of peace, and apologized for almost knocking the table over. It wasn't enough.

The boy jumped up. Everybody else froze. I kept walking.

"Hey," he shouted at me. I had gone but three steps. I stopped and turned. He was glowering.

"Yeah, man, what?"

"Why don't you go around?" he said. "You don't be stepping through my shit like that."

Again, I said I was sorry. Still it wasn't enough. Now he had a point to prove, and I could tell he had a point to prove by the way he kept looking at the friends around him.

"Naw, man," he said. "Sorry don't cut it."

I walked straight to him then. I stood over him and he who had felt himself in command now was nervous.

"What's it going to be then?" I asked him. "What more do you need?"

He didn't say a word. He felt the threat I posed and skipped any intermediate stages that might normally have filled the next few moments. He went straightaway far from the realm of reason. He lifted the bottom of his sweatshirt and revealed to me the pistol he had stuck in the waistband of his baggy pants. He never pulled the gun. He simply showed it to me—as if showing it would be enough.

It is one of the gestures, it seems, of the streets nowadays. I had first seen it from the window of my apartment. A fight had broken out in the street below, and I had stuck my head out to listen more closely, and of course to watch the action. I have no idea what the fight was about, don't know who won. Possibly there was no real winner. There was no real action. There was only a lot of shouting until one young man lifted the tail of his shirt and showed the gun.

"Come on, then," he shouted in his final series of taunting. "You want some of this?" That's when he exposed himself. That's when he showed the pistol.

The other man backed down, backed away, turned away, walked away.

I thought at the time that, if ever facing a similar situation, a similar pistol stuck in a similar waistband and a similar offer to back down, I would have backed down too. It was the prudent thing to do, the easy thing to do. But when my turn came, I all of a sudden didn't think anymore that the easy way was the best way.

Perhaps after all, when my turn finally came, and it was upon me now, I simply stopped thinking, wasn't thinking at all, in fact. I was just feeling.

I looked at the pistol. I looked at the man behind the thing. He was just a boy. He was, like my young buddy Henry, far too young to die, this youngster, this young gangster, this child who was some mother's son and far too young to die in the wars that raged nowadays in these streets. He would never live to be an older man if someone didn't teach him a different way.

It didn't have to be me who taught him. I would have preferred that it not be. I would have preferred not to have been on that street on that particular day, when and where a boy too young to have a legal drink in a bar had the power of serious injury and even the power of life and death over me. I would have preferred to have been at home, an iced bucket of champagne beside my bed, a little osetra caviar and smoked Nova Scotia salmon to tide me over until dinner. But there I was. I had been chosen to teach him.

It didn't have to be much. He merely had to learn that he had a choice.

I wasn't thinking any of this at the time. Of course not! You don't have but a second and a half to come up with a course of action before one is thrust upon you. It is better, I have found, to do the thrusting yourself.

"What are you going to do with that thing?" I said. "Are you going to shoot me? Or are you just trying to scare me?" He only glowered.

"Look, man," I said. "Any pussy with a pistol can scare somebody. Hell, any pussy with a pistol can shoot somebody too. It's no big deal."

I took the last step toward him. He stepped back.

"What else you got?" I asked him. "Is this what you're about? Is this *all* you're about? What do you do when the gun's empty?"

Until now this youngster perhaps had never been asked to consider. Maybe he had never been offered any choices, and he did what he did and he was who he was in large part because the world seemed so ordained for him, so circumscribed. He did what everyone around him did—no more, no less.

Perhaps there had been no one to tell him that his world did not have to resemble an anthropological study, and that it did not have to devolve into some kind of Darwinian microcosm in which impulsive violence reigns almost as a survival tool: an avenue, it can be said, to status.

A shot at survival: that seems to be, in an anthropological sense, what it is all about, all of it, a chance to survive. We're talking here about a type of survival that is different from personal survival and has to do more with something that is locked away in our genes, a tendency toward survival of the fittest—which is not to say best or brightest or strongest or bravest, but which has to do entirely, it seems, with the attainment of those almost arbitrary things of a given place and era which afford an increase in mating opportunities. By mating often, anthropological man and the apes exhibit what lie deeply embedded in the genetic makeup: the desire and perhaps the need to survive to the next round. The genes that survive are the genes of this game's winners.

The triumphant, of course, are those men who win in the competition for reproductive success. That's what it is all about: access to women, genetic survival. Plainly put, then, life among men is a contest for women, and the winner wins not with muscle, money or might, although these might be part of the equation and at various times certainly have been. The winner wins with status.

In every human society, as in the society of chimps, males compete with one another for status. To gain and guard respect are among the desperate desires of men and manhood, and a man will go very far indeed to be a Man, to exhibit his manhood, to earn respect and to counter and avenge any signs and acts of disrespect directed at him. This in large measure explains the threat of violence that seems to hover forever near in the interaction of men, violence that cannot always be labeled and brushed aside as social pathology. It is what men do. Reproductive success depends on it.

What I knew then, of course, was what I knew from long ago: when you find a man who has killed a man he knows, chances are that the murder took place in front of witnesses. Violence, it seems, often requires an audience.

On the street that afternoon, we were not alone, this boy and I. His friends were there with him. They were watching and listening when I said the things I said to him, and their presence worried me more than anything else. On these streets the war rages in part because so little else exists to reinforce a man's image of himself. Respect and reputation are as important as they are anywhere else. In fact it can be argued that respect and reputation are everything, since there *is* so little else. Status is hardly secured in the same ways as it is in the outside world. The rules are different here. Words are weapons. Every slight is an insult. An insignificant dispute can lead to a beating, can lead to a killing, and a man is a man only if he can stand up and back up his words with action. The threat of violence runs through every encounter.

My young man could easily have felt his reputation under siege by the way I spoke to him. But if I backed down now, my respectability would have vanished. Without meaning to, without thinking, I had managed to back him and me into a corner.

He had possibly never had anyone to teach him that he didn't have to do what the others might do, or what they might have him do, that he could create a world and a way of his own. Maybe there had been no one to tell him how; no one to give him a sense of himself, no one to demand of him that he be unafraid—no one simply to demand of him what he would not think to demand of himself. For both our sakes, I wished someone in his younger life had showed him. Since there hadn't been, it looked like I had been chosen to be that someone.

"You don't have to use that thing," I said to him. "You don't have to be afraid not to."

By the look on his face, I had now confused him.

"Just hold it for a second," I told him. "And think about what I just said. You can pull that pistol and you can use it, or you can not use it. Whatever you choose, it's your choice, so think about it first. And whatever you do, don't do it because you're afraid not to."

He stood motionless for a long moment. Slowly he relaxed and let his shirttail cover over the butt of his pistol. He didn't shoot me.

It could be that his cooler nature had prevailed. It could also be that I had perplexed him. Or maybe I had gotten him to think for just a second, to try and find a better way than the instinctive way. A better way? I don't really know, but at least a different way. The different ways are the ways that most people don't try. They are the ways maybe that need to be taught.

I came to this realization one night in autumn—my first autumn. I was only a witness. Nothing happened to me that night, in fact nothing happened very much at all that night. I was simply walking home. It wasn't so very late, somewhere between twelve-thirty and one o'clock in the morning. Three women were gabbing in front of the apartment building where they lived at the corner of Convent and 128th. A young child was riding a bicycle in the middle of the street. The bike was a little too big for the kid, he was a little awkward on it, and a car was coming. It came slowly enough. There seemed to be no immediate danger, but all of a sudden the mother of the cycling child screamed.

"Get your ass out that street," she cried, and the little kid panicked at the suddenness of the mother's shrieking. He pedaled as fast as he could and aimed his bike for the sidewalk and hit the curb. He nearly fell, and I laughed a little.

My thoughts as I strolled that night had been a thousand miles to the west. All at once I was brought back to Harlem. All at once I noticed that this kid was not the only kid on this street at one o'clock in the morning. There were four or five others. These were their mothers, these women chatting on the street. And the children were playing nearby.

At noon, or at six in the evening, it would have been a pleasant scene, the kind of homey snapshot that might grace a small community's church calendar. As it was, I had thought nothing of it at first, for the scene was an all too common one in Harlem, even at this late hour: children playing, mothers hanging out, everyone watching everyone else's children. But for some reason the lateness of the night hit me then, and I wondered why this woman was yelling at this child for playing in the street when the child, to my way of thinking, ought not to have been out playing anywhere at that hour—not in the street, not on the side-walk, not anywhere. Tomorrow was a school day. That kid and all those kids should have been in the house, in bed, fast asleep.

But then, the mothers would have had to sacrifice their night out on the stoop. And then again, someone would have had to make a connection between sleep and rest and per-formance in class, and a further connection between perfor-mance in class and escape. Still again, someone would have had to care enough to care enough.

Wilma Bishop informed me one time that caring isn't easy. The asperity in her voice grated the nerve edges of my heart.

"Sometimes," she said, "it's easier to forget than to care. And it gets easier and easier, until—you know—finally you just forget how. That's how it goes when you feel trapped."

Four little girls, one of them hers, were jumping rope on the sidewalk in front of an apartment on 139th Street. I had stopped to watch them. The rhythm of the swinging rope, the lilt of the ditty they chanted, transported me back to my long-ago childhood when I would stand and watch the girls and never get invited to take a turn. I have never jumped rope on the street.

From the days when I was very very small I have been an admirer of rope jumpers, double-dutchers, those girls who could toss themselves into the eggbeater blades of two ropes held at the ends by two companions, who turned each rope in an opposite direction from the outside in. Sometimes both ropes were held at one end by only one companion, the other ends tied to a rail, or one long rope looped around a street lamp. Girls when I was young would jump rope for hours and hours, and I would watch them and never get a chance to play.

I used to watch the girls when the other boys in my neighborhood had gone into the alley to shoot basketballs into a hoop nailed to someone's garage door. While they imagined themselves stars in a crowded arena, I watched the girls who did what they did for the love of it, for the fun of it, stepping briskly to the rhythms of the turning ropes, reciting the words of some singsongy ditty and counting the number of successful passes of the rope. And I would be mesmerized.

The girls before me that day in Harlem held hypnotic sway over me in the same way as the jump-roping girls of those old days, and I stood watching them for twenty minutes before Wilma came out to keep an eye on me, who kept an eye on the young girls. To put Wilma at ease, I walked to where she stood and sat at her feet on the little stoop.

I told her I liked watching little girls jump rope. She eyed me with suspicion.

"Um-hum," she said. "Lots of men like watching little girls. You live around here?"

I told her where. I said I was just out for a walk, and we chatted for a few minutes. She relaxed a little, but she never surrendered her vigilance.

She reminded me somehow of those simpler days of my not so long ago childhood and of the women who prowl my memories, a lifetime ago surely, although it seems more like a hundred years or more have passed, so much has changed. Yet here was Wilma Bishop like some neighbor lady out of my past, a somewhat kinder time, it seemed, when young children were watched, when the neighbor ladies kept an eye on us all. They would yell at us if we stepped out of line. They would report to our parents the crimes we had committed. They would open their doors to us and bandage us when we fell too hard and left the skin of our knees on the sidewalk. If our moms weren't home, there was always a neighbor lady that we could run crying to. We didn't always like it, I'm sure, those neighborly eyes all the time spying on us. Nor could we possibly have come close to appreciating what those neighbor ladies meant to us. But no matter. Even if we didn't like it, even if we didn't appreciate it, even if we didn't altogether know it, we were safe on the streets of our neighborhood in those days. Someone was always on the lookout, always watching over us, the same as

Wilma Bishop was doing with her kids and with the kids of her neighbors.

"Someone has to do it," she said to me. "It's not easy to care anymore, but somebody has to."

Her words rang out with the magic of an incantation and hung for a long time like dust in the air. Wilma's voice was the voice of a sorcerer casting a spell, and the spell came back to haunt me again and again. I heard her voice, I heard her words, I remembered them, I thought about them often. They slipped into my ears as I walked home that night and watched and heard the young mother screaming at her child for playing in the street. They formed the far-away echo I heard when Eliot Winston with an incantation of his own bid me to turn round and approach him. They still had their sting that night, that early morning, when I peered into the darkness outside my window and saw the man beating the woman, when I knew there was a choice to make and I made it.

So dramatic it sounds, as if some great battle were raging inside my head, as if I were about to do something wildly out of character, something noble and heroic. But no. What I did that night was no more virtuous, no more courageous than wearing white silk trousers and lavender or salmon-colored shirts and walking the streets of Harlem. In fact, they were the same thing to me.

One day I will realize that there is nothing I can do about anything that truly matters, or that perhaps there is simply nothing to be done about anything because nothing at all really matters. I will continue to tell myself that I care about Harlem and about black people, of course, but from that moment on I will look only inward. And in that moment, Harlem will have happened to me.

I will stall that moment's arrival for as long as I can. I will refuse for now to surrender more than I already have.

I looked into my closet and considered the shirts and the silk trousers with the same sensation of defeat with which I looked from my window that late night and early morning. It was the same sensation that pricked me when the woman screamed and startled the kid on the bike, the same again that was with me when I overheard Eliot saying, "The black man is finished." There was a choice to make—in the closet, on the street: a choice to make.

Life is all about choice, I have decided, life and the predicaments we find ourselves in. It is all about what we have chosen or not chosen, and about what others have chosen for us.

Whether we realize it or ever even notice, someone has made for us—very often we, ourselves, have made them; very often not—the choices that seemingly affect our every breath, our every thought, and all that we do or try, and all that we are. And we are left, as a result of all the choices taken or not taken, in a way, rather choiceless.

As I watched the mother that night and the child who nearly fell from the bike, the child who ought to have been asleep in bed; as I looked up and down the avenue and up and down each street I crossed as I was walking home that night, and every time I set foot after that night onto the streets of Harlem; as I witness the man beating the woman outside my window; as I listen to Wilma Bishop and think of Eliot Winston and his brother T.C., of Hans Hegeman and Ann Plymouth and Wilson Clark; I can see, more clearly than I can see anything else, that absence of choice is the active ingredient in surrender. When what is becomes in the mind what will be, when the heart tells you that this is how it is, that this is the way things are and the way things are going to be, then what's the use in fighting? What's the use in trying? The game is up and there is nothing left, no pain no joy no satisfaction, nothing but the look of the surrender and the resignation that Wilma Bishop seeks every day to avoid.

"Someone has to care," she said. "Someone has to sit out here on this stoop and on these streets and keep an eye on these children. Someone has to make sure they get something to eat at suppertime and make sure they go to bed at bedtime and make sure they go to school in the morning. And somebody has got to care about how they're doing in school. Somebody has got to do all these things if for no other reason than to show these children out here that somebody cares. Not just about them, but that somebody cares about something. Anything. Otherwise, what they see all the time is what they'll get stuck with. And all they see every day is that nobody cares about them or about much of anything else either. So why should *they*? The poorest ones, the saddest ones, the ones who need the most caring of all, they're the ones nobody cares for or looks out for. And they're the ones it's easiest to lose. If you don't care about these little children, pretty soon they don't care about themselves. And when they stop caring about themselves, they stop caring about you, and it doesn't take long before they don't care about much of anything."

There was a fire suddenly lit in her eyes, and I thought all the tears in the world would never put it out.

"And that's where we are now, goddamn it!" she said, and said it so loudly, so violently that the world's heart skipped a beat then, but only for a second. One of the girls turning the rope lost her rhythm. You could hear it in the way the rope slapped at the pavement. The girl at the other end lost her hold. The rope slipped from her fingers. The girl jumping got tangled up. For a second it seemed that nothing moved, and nothing did. Wilma had snared the attention of all the girls and all within earshot, and they all stared, a little startled.

Surely on these streets they had heard stronger language and anger. This was more.

They looked, the girls did, and then went back to their playing. Everything was back to normal. Wilma again put the lid on the kettle where it belonged, where it had been for such a long time, and where for a long time it had contained the pressure building up, which cried out for release but could find no outlet. Now the seal had been broken, and Wilma hissed like steam escaping.

"It *is* a prison here, goddamn it. It *is* a prison," she said. "A prison of the mind, a prison of the spirit. And we're all trapped in it together. It doesn't matter whether we live in Harlem or in the backwoods of Kentucky somewhere. We are all caught up in the same prison, but they can't—none of them—see it. And it never seems to occur to them how it's all connected and that something needs to be done. They just hurry on past and keep their eyes closed and act like they can't see the ones who are crying."

They cry invisible tears—the ones you hear rather than see, or if you see them, they are the kind you see not on the face but in the way lives are lived.

I do not know to whom her plea was directed, for I never asked her, but it *was* a plea, that much is clear, the same lament that has been echoing in the souls of black folks in America since the beginning and that will continue as long as the isolation continues.

It is the isolation that makes the prison, of course, and as with all prisons there is confinement on both sides of the fence. We hold our positions like some kind of army encamped and we guard ourselves against the outsiders, against all the ones who are not like us, the others among us, for *we* are this one thing (I am one thing, you and I

2 4 5

together are this one thing, we are Jews, we are black, we are Christians, we are white, we are Americans, we are whole—whatever that means), and they are *those other people.* And we don't want them near us, don't want them included in these things that are ours.

Thus we must be ever on guard against them, build for ourselves mighty fortresses with many defenses in place. After a time, it becomes difficult to tell who are the imprisoned.

Until, that is, you come to Harlem and you see what some have been left with, and what some have settled for.

I walked one afternoon across 135th and turned south onto Fifth Avenue—the same Fifth Avenue that downtown is crowded with shops and shoppers and yellow cabs and is all hustle and bustle and business. It is the same Fifth Avenue, but it is a different world.

A woman approached me as I neared 129th Street. She smiled, greeted me like an old friend, stopped me, and started talking. She said, "You're looking mighty handsome today," and I thought maybe I had met her before and just didn't remember. It was a nice day, she said, she was feeling better, she said, she hoped good fortune was smiling on me. Then she asked me for a quarter.

A quarter!

I know that quarters add up, and if you bum enough of them you, like Pig Foot Mary, could turn a little into a lot, even into a fortune. But the woman could have asked for a dollar, or a couple of bucks, or she could have said, "Can you help me out with some spare change?" I don't know why, but to ask for twenty-five cents seemed such a desperate request that I just felt sad.

Another day, another street, another woman. Gaunt and ghostly, she hardly seemed human, and was so frail a stiff wind would have blown her down. Her skin hung like limp clothing from her bones, and there were gaps where her teeth had fallen out. But she sashayed—or tried to—as she walked toward me, her pathetic grin twisting her face into a hideous grimace. She offered me the use of her body for two dollars.

Two small dollars.

For food, for a drink, for a vial of crack cocaine: it doesn't matter for what. There was in her eye such a look of desperation and submission that I could scarcely contain my disappointment. I looked at her and I looked in my memory and I looked up and down every street and avenue in Harlem, and in that briefest of moments I remembered every black man I had ever seen standing with nothing to do on some street corner and every embittered black woman with a baby in her arms or in the street or clutched to her hip. They were present there in this woman's eyes.

In the book of Exodus there is a passage that came to me, the Pharaoh's decree that *"Every boy that is born shall be thrown into the Nile, but let every girl live."* I can see daily the drowning of the men and wonder at the myth that the women were allowed to live. It seems they were hurled into the Nile to die as well, for how can you kill the one without taking the life of the other?

The jobless, prospectless men on every corner; the

women begging for drug money; the child biking in the street at all hours of the night; the rats and the roaches and all the signs of poverty and degradation that have been settled for and that pass for living here: it is no wonder that Eliot Winston insists that black folk are finished, that they have, in general, given up the game and surrendered. Who in the face of such continuing gloom would not be ready to quit?

I was ready myself to give up, as ready as I would be that night and early morning to believe what I have been told and taught about black people and about being black, ready then to turn my back and walk away once and for all from all that black has become and is and means, ready once more to leave Harlem, to seek out the quiet life in some out-of-the-way place far from here and never look back.

Perhaps my father wasn't fooling after all when he told us that we were Jewish. Perhaps he meant it literally, perhaps he didn't, but in terms of historical oppression and revulsion there are so many parallels between the one people and the other that they might as well be the same people. And when the seder Haggadah tells us that "our history moves from slavery toward freedom. Our narration begins with degradation and rises to dignity," it might easily be referring to the plight of black people in America.

But where is the rise to dignity?

Perhaps the black man, the black woman, have given up, are finished, are through, are dead.

Eliot's death of the black man is different from mine. When I think of this death, when I think of the world my father must have been hoping for, when I think of myself and the way I am in the world, I think in terms of victory. I think of a time when the black man will be able to die to himself and reemerge in glory, to move beyond the horrors of the past and into a world where he can participate fully, and not just in the segregated sections set aside for him and that he too often ends up settling for.

It used to be that if we weren't allowed to play we would knock on the doors loudly enough and persistently enough, make enough noise and commotion until we were finally let in. Now it seems that if we aren't allowed to play, we'll take what crumbs we're given and just go home, piss on them and make a paste and hurl them at someone.

Eliot disagrees that blacks have given up the struggle, that we've ceased making trouble. He says that every act of surrender, every drug deal, every act of violence, is a hammering against the protective coating of an insensitive society.

"Every bit of pounding," he said, "dents their sense of safety, and people start to think everything is caving in around them. And it is. And we got to keep on pounding until they'll realize that what goes on in here has an effect on what goes on out there. It's like Malcolm X said: 'We got to make them see that we are the enemy. We got to make them turn their defense money on us and either destroy us or cure the conditions that brought our people to this point.'"

We were still walking down Park Avenue with a view into the two faces of American life. Eliot had calmed down.

"We got to keep pounding until they start to take us seriously, until they start to care about us and what happens here," he said. "As it is now, they only pay attention to us because all the demons that terrorize their sense of safety have gotten completely out of control and they don't know what to do. Everything's coming apart all around them, but the white folks are so stupid they still think they can fix what's wrong with the country without dealing with the statistical realities that define a large part of black life and culture—certainly in their eyes, since it's the most visible aspect of present-day Harlem: the drugs and the crime and the poverty and the rats and the apathy and the despair that plague our community. It's the saddest and the most tragic part, that's for sure, and that's all they can see. Hell, sometimes it's all I can see too."

He let a large puff of air escape from the strong statue that he was, and he seemed to deflate. As long as he maintained a certain tension, a certain anger, he stood tall and he scowled and he was fierce. The minute he let himself admit to the apparent hopelessness of the situation, he weakened. The breath he exhaled seemed to carry with it Eliot's intensity, almost his very soul. I thought he might cry.

It was as if a sinister pall had been draped over him, the same one that has been draped over the landscape of Harlem, over its life and over its spirit.

"We've been deprived of light and air for so long," Eliot said. "The hope that once sustained us, the hope that one day we as a people would get to the promised land, has been pretty much extinguished here. Maybe it was naive to hope that we could someday—all of us; not just black people—be judged by the content of our hearts, like Dr. King said, and not by the color of our skin. Wouldn't it be nice if we weren't so limited by the abjectness of our circumstance, if our fates were not so subject to the whims of white people? Why can't our destinies lie in what we choose to do for ourselves? Isn't that what they promised us, that given the right amount of effort, the right amount of perseverance and, yeah, even the right amount of luck, we could indeed strive and achieve, live any life and be anything we set our hearts firmly enough on? But it's a lie. Who has persevered any more than black people? Who has worked harder and for less reward than we have? Maybe it's the luck part, because we have been damned sure unlucky."

He tried to muster a laugh. He couldn't find it.

"We only had the one hope," he said. "We just wanted to be treated fairly. We just wanted to be given the unimpeded opportunity to succeed. But every time, man, they closed every door we tried to step into. The promise that patience would win the day, that tomorrow would be better than today. Man, that promise has been broken time and time again. The dream deferred from one generation to the next has not come true. Life has not gotten better, or even remained the same; it's gotten worse. The hope here on the streets of Harlem has been smothered and snuffed out. Our hope has been erased.

"That's why we think so small," he said. "We think we've accomplished something great by making a record and singing and dancing on TV. That's what we think of when we think of success, singers and basketball players. If we can't do that, we self-destruct because we got nothing else. Even when we can do that, we get caught up in drugs and all kinds of stupid traps. And that's the saddest part of all. That pounding we're doing, all that noise we think we're making, all those acts of violence, all the drugging and the robbing and all the rest of it, it might be waking up the white man, but mostly what we're doing is destroying ourselves."

He looked away and stuck his hands in his pockets.

"Man," he said. "It's hopeless."

It's hopeless, he said. It's hopeless.

It's hopeless.

It's hopeless.

It's hopeless.

The echo was startling.

"It's hopeless," he said. "And there is nothing we can do about it."

This was the Eliot Winston who when I first saw him was brimming with bravado. Even as we walked up Park Avenue he seemed a pillar of rage. He was preaching against the white man, hurling abuse at a system that because of its injustice was collapsing under the weight of its oppression. And now here he was ready to sign off.

"No," I said. "You're wrong." That's all I said. I thought it as I looked at Eliot and listened to him: the black man *is* dead, but as much as I longed—and still long, in fact—to see the death of the black man, it is a different death of which I speak and for which I yearn for all black men. It is the death of what the black man has come to symbolize. It is a death signifying glorious resurrection and rebirth.

He stared into my eyes for another long moment, and when he took his eyes away from mine he looked me up and down. His grin was half smile, half pursed lips of forced patience, the look one gives a child acting silly. He gave a little snort and a *hmph.*

"I hope you're right," he said. "I hope you're right."

He held out his hand to me and we shook. A tense moment had passed.

"I hope so too," I said. "I hope so too."

All around us there were the signs of surrender, staring us in the face, impossible to miss, impossible to avoid, everywhere surfacing and resurfacing, no matter how swell a street, no matter how prosperous a neighborhood, no matter how upscale and mobile, no matter how vibrant, no matter how tough talking and cool.

And here was Eliot, not just that day on the corner, but this day too on Park Avenue, a marathon runner out of wind, out of leg, out of life; an until-death-do-us-part partner who just can't go the distance anymore.

And here was his brother T.C., who had made a career of smashing windows to vent his frustration—car windows, shop windows, any window he thought belonged to someone white—and slugging white people to vent his rage, and who in the end was afraid that he would take a hammer and steal at random into the homes of white people and bash their heads in. He had been to prison twice already. He didn't want to go back. He came to Harlem instead, to hide, he said, because he couldn't take the outside world any longer. He gave up.

Wilson Clark too, now that I think of it, had given up, had come to Harlem because he felt a deep need to be in a place that was his, not *theirs.*

Wilson had long known the myth of Harlem and had

been seduced by it. He had heard of the magic of Harlem in stories his grandfather had told him, rumors whispered in old movies, the glory of Harlem that, even if it no longer existed, could still be felt along the streets and avenues where the restless spirits of the past still wander.

"I used to tell myself," he once said to me, "that I was coming to Harlem to live among the spirits of our past. You know? It's like how ghosts have to wander restlessly as long as the lives they led lack some kind of completion. A man who's been murdered or a body that's not been properly buried: they can't pass to the next world, to the next life, until things are settled for them in this one. It's the unfinished business that does it. But I never suspected that by coming to Harlem I would be giving up. I thought I was coming here to save myself, to escape that look in white folks' eyes, sure, but to save myself, to be among my people, to be where I could feel safe from that look. You know that look. It's the look that says 'This world is ours and everything that's in it. And you, black man, you've got no right to any part of it except what we grant you.' It's that white-people look, and sometimes it's panic, and sometimes it's arrogance, and sometimes it's a threat. You've seen it a thousand times, and if you stick around, you'll see it a thousand times again. Well, I got tired of that look. I didn't want to see it anymore. I came to Harlem to get away from it."

He took a sip of beer. (We were in the bar where we had met, near the corner of 125th and Morningside.)

"But its hot gaze reaches all the way up here," he said.

"Maybe you feel it even more up here, because here you cannot fool yourself. Here you can really see just how separate the two worlds are: the one world where people believe that playing by the rules will get them somewhere closer to their dreams; and this other world where there is hardly any dreaming done and playing by the rules is meaningless. There are no rules here—not that the other America would recognize anyway."

Wilson looked up from the glass of beer he had been staring into since he began. He turned briefly to me and then looked away. He caught his own reflection in the mirror behind the bar and stared for a long time at himself.

"I didn't realize it when I came here," he said. "I was just so thrilled to be coming here and then to finally get here. Man, that's all I thought I needed was to get here with the black folks, away from white people. Let them have the rest, let them have it all, I said to myself. Let them have it all. Now I know that when I let that look drive me almost out of my mind, when I let that look force me to come to live in Harlem, I was letting the white folks win. And I was letting my grandfather down."

I thought he was going to cry. He stared at himself in the mirror without blinking until his eyes watered. He clenched his fist around his beer glass tighter and tighter until his arm quivered. Suddenly all tension left him, and his spirit slumped from fatigue. He was weary, physically and emotionally, about as tired as I have ever seen anyone.

I can understand his fatigue. And Eliot's fatigue. And T.C.'s. I have felt it too. Sometimes I just want to run and hide, move to the south of France and sip champagne all day, far from the field of battle. I just want to put my feet up and relax.

And suppose I did. So what? Suppose I retreated, turned my back once more and concerned myself with only me. What then? Would it be such a great loss?

I can't help but think of a man who lived in my childhood neighborhood. I don't know his name. I'm not even sure I knew his name then. But he bought a shiny new Cadillac and parked it on the street in front of his house. On Saturday afternoons, when the weather was nice, out in front of the house he'd be, stripped to his shorts, a bucket of soapy water in one hand, a rag or a sponge in the other. Every week he washed that car. He kept it shiny. He kept it looking new.

The car sparked a bit of envy, I'm sure. It had those big tailfins of the late 1950s, and it had electric windows and an air conditioner. It was the talk of the neighborhood, even after it was no longer new. It always looked good. It was well cared for. It was a thing of beauty, a kind of monument.

The car became community property. The car was *our* car, the neighborhood's car, and the kids would lean against it when the man wasn't looking, before he could come out of the house and chase us all away. Then he would walk down to the car and check for any damage we had done and wipe away the smudges and smears with a cloth he always carried. We would hide behind lampposts and other parked cars to watch him, and then lean again on the car when he had gone back inside. He could chase us away, but the minute his back was turned, it was our car again, something all the kids on the block took a little pride in.

In retrospect it wasn't much, having a Cadillac on the block, not really such a big deal. And neither was having Bob Gibson, who lived across the hall from us. He was a rookie pitcher with the baseball team the year he moved in, and we scarcely knew him, but somehow he and the man with the Cadillac meant something to us, just to have them near, just to be able to look at them and say: "Those men, what they do, where they go, and what they have: they come from here. Where they go, we go. What they have, we have. For they are us."

Without a word, just being there, they offered us—I don't want to say they offered us something to aspire to, for a fancy car is no big deal, nor is being a sports star, but they offered us choice, a way to be that we could accept or reject. There was choice.

I looked into my closet and I pulled out the silk trousers and the lavender shirt.

When I was a small boy, the black men I knew always seemed to dress well, maybe even better than they could afford to dress. They always looked good, always had a certain style about them. I never knew why, never even questioned. Now I believe they were making a statement. Dressing well, looking good: these were more than matters of taste and habit. They were acts of defiance that showed in the way the men walked, in the way they talked, in the clothes they wore. There was a sense of dignity in the way they carried themselves, in how they showed themselves to the world.

It has never been easy to be black in this country. You had to do some small thing—many things, in fact, large and small—to keep hammering, to keep surrender one more day away.

Dressing well wasn't much, perhaps—you cannot save the world, I know, with the clothes you wear—but it was something. Probably with such silly things you cannot offer much hope either, but you do what you can, no matter how small, no matter how ridiculous, to keep the cruelty of the beast at bay. And maybe—just maybe—you can offer a little choice to those who seem to have none. It takes a certain naïveté to believe in hope, to believe that the world can be changed, that the world one day *will* be changed.

Nowadays the young men of Harlem dress as if to hide themselves. They wear costumes of cool and suits of rebellion, hooded sweatshirts, baggy pants, shoes big enough to drown in. It is an effort, it seems, to speak in a loud and angry voice to the rest of the world, but with their hoods up, their shoulders hunched, shuffling low as they walk, they seem as well to be hiding, trying hard to be invisible to a world that already ignores them. They seem to have lost the naïveté to believe in hope. In fact they seem to have lost hope itself.

There is a look in the eye that says it, that says the hope is all but gone. It is the look of resignation and surrender. It is the look that says, This is how it is. It is the look of bitter disappointment and shame, the look of being ashamed for mankind if this *is* in fact how things are and how they are going to be.

It is the look that Johnny Cannon wore, the look that stared back from the mirror at Wilson Clark, the look, I'm sure, of the man who beats the woman outside my window. It was the look that Eliot Wilson was about to put on, not that day on the corner by the Metro North station, but that day as we walked up Park Avenue. He was almost tired enough to put it on, but not quite yet. His naïveté had almost left him, the same as it had already left the woman whose kid rode his bike in the street at one in the morning. She no longer seemed to care.

As I think back over my time in Harlem, I remember very clearly the expression of the woman who had offered to lend her body to me in exchange for two dollars. It haunts me. I see it in my dreams, that look in her eyes. I think of it, oddly enough, not as a ghostly warning of death. In her eyes there was despair, that is certain. There was also a tiny light I could not see at the time, and in my memory it shines faintly, but distinctly, not a dim light fading out, but a dim light trying to come back on. She may have given up, but she was fighting to get the light back on, fighting to get back into the game. She was not through yet. There was still a bit of naïveté within her. It may not have been in her eyes, but it was in her walk. I cannot forget how she sashayed when she walked toward me, how she tried to look alluring and desirable. You have to start somewhere. And then you do what you can.

I keep thinking of Hans Hegeman. I think of Wilma Bishop too, sitting on the front stoop, watching, caring, showing those children playing that she cares. *Someone* has to care, she told me. Someone has to stay and watch over them.

And I think of Ann Plymouth, who, so she says, likes to have me and my funny clothes around.

"It's not just the clothes," she told me. "It's you and where you're going, it's you and where you've been. When you come around, you light up my child's world with the stories you tell. You let her know that the world she sees every day is not all there is."

Ann had reprimanded me once for my coming here and pretending to be poor.

"No, that is not your value here," she said. "We already know how to be poor. We don't need somebody from the outside coming here and feeling all sorry for us and everything. We don't need somebody coming up here to tell us that the world out there doesn't mean anything and that we shouldn't want what we don't already have. What we need is somebody to show us that there *is* a world out there and it's our world too and that we should not settle so easily and so blindly for this one. That's what I need you for. That's what my child needs you for. Otherwise we are doing just fine without you."

Ann Plymouth opened my eyes, and when I looked more closely I could see that all is not death and dying in Harlem, all is not surrender. Harlem has other heroes too who have remained and continue to fight, or who left and returned. Harlem has other patron saints who stand on the pedestal beside Pig Foot Mary. There are the thousand stories you hear of men and women like Bessie Delany, a Harlem dentist who during the Great Depression gave food to those of her patients who were hungry and had no money, and who in twenty-seven years as a dentist for the poor people of Harlem never once raised her rates; and the many others like her, some that we've all heard of, the countless others who are nameless to us. They all, like Pig Foot Mary, had a choice. Bessie Delany elected to stay.

Hans Hegeman had the same choice as Bessie Delany, the choice to leave or stay. He got out. He had been born in Harlem and raised in Harlem, but he had gotten onto the pathway that leads out and away from Harlem. He had gone to an elite boys' academy called Collegiate School, and went on to Princeton University and to law school at Columbia. He got a job as a corporate lawyer, he worked in the district attorney's office, he worked for the public defender. None of these jobs, however, fit who he was. After a while none of them, he said, made any sense. It wasn't what he felt comfortable doing, so with his brother Ivan he came back to Harlem and started an after-school program in the yard, in fact, of the very building where he and Ivan had lived as boys.

The program was initially designed to give kids in the neighborhood a place to be instead of on the streets with the dope sellers and the users. Eventually it grew into an alternative school program. There are more than just a few of these programs in Harlem, attempting, all of them, to do what the public schools have failed to do. They call them storefront schools.

I asked Hans Hegeman to give me a job. He did. He gave me a chance to do what little I could. It wasn't much, but it was the finest thing I have ever done.

Two times a week I went to help out in the after-school program. Most of the kids stay until the early evening. The extra two hours gives them a little more time in a safe place, less time on the streets, still more time to learn something new. I offered a writing class to twelve- and thirteen-year-olds and helped them find ways to express themselves on paper.

When I first got them, three or four lines of writing was all I could coax out of them. By year's end, it was difficult to get them to stop when each session was over.

It was to this school, East Harlem School at Exodus House, that I was headed when I met Eliot Winston for the first time. Now when I think of Eliot, I think always of Hans Hegeman.

"Our mission," Hans told me, "extends beyond formal education. Our roots are here in the community, so we know the narrowness of this world. A lot of these kids would never think to go below Ninety-sixth Street just to walk around or have a look or go to a museum. It's got to be a school trip, and that's only a once-or-twice-a-year thing. To them it's a completely different world down there below Ninety-sixth Street, another strange group of people they've had no opportunity to figure out. They don't bother us, so we don't bother them: that's how they feel. Most of them don't go into any type of analysis, wondering how the people downtown affect the situation up here. They don't have the luxury and they don't have the desire to engage in that kind of thinking."

And it seems the folks downtown don't have the desire either.

"People downtown only think about these things at election time or when there's a problem," Hans said. "For most people downtown, the people up here are the others. These are sweet wonderful kids, but the folks downtown don't make the effort to find them. The folks downtown don't go out of their way to do anything for them. Unless somebody cares—unless we care—they'll all just get lost."

He seems not to be a sentimental man. He makes deals with the drug dealers on the street so the kids can walk to school unmolested.

"If these kids had some way of finding out about the wider world out there, they might get the shot at it," he said. "But man, it's hard. It's incredible to me the hoops I have still to jump through at the age of thirty-five with two Ivy League degrees just to get anything accomplished, and it's scary to me knowing what they're going to have to face. And they'll need every single advantage they can possibly get."

Hans Hegeman. Ann Plymouth. Wilma Bishop.

There is a choice to make; there is always a choice.

We like our choices and decisions to seem like great battles that rage within us, as if what we write are epics to last the ages, as if by what we do and think we carry the weight of the universe upon our shoulders.

I look from my window and I think that maybe it's true, that maybe white silk trousers are important, that maybe what I am about to do will have a huge impact on the destinies of mankind. So I would like to believe, but we do what we do, I think—no matter what we tell ourselves and one another, no matter what we pretend—we do what we do to save our own poor souls. We do what we do because it's who we are.

I looked from my window, that night of nights, and it all crystallized before me, and the darkness provided for me a moment of calm, despite the jumble that had been made of my thoughts and feelings, despite all I had seen and done, heard and felt, despite what I knew I was about to do. The darkness provided for me a moment of utter clarity. I looked out through the shadow of that late night and early morning, and for a long second there was rage—rage enough to be blinded by.

A man was beating a woman.

In the few moments of my indecision I told myself that enough was enough, told myself that I wanted no longer to be black if this is how black men behaved, told myself that I wanted nothing more to do with a world without beauty in it, and that cared not for beauty. It had been beautiful and joyful once, but this—this man beating this woman—this is what we've let it all come down to: this man beating this woman, the drug dealers lining too many streets in the neighborhood, women willing to sell themselves for a pittance and men willing to buy them, the rats and the roaches, the joblessness, the fatherless children and the mothers who do not care, the far too many people who do not seem to care.

I told myself that I refused to be black—as if I really could, as if I am black because of the color of my skin, because of the things I do, and not instead because of the ways in which the world sees and reacts to and treats that color.

I refused to be black, as if there were freedom in that refusal, as if by rejecting I could likewise reject any responsibility I might have, as if I were an island not at all connected beneath the surface to the lands all around me.

I refused to be black because suddenly I could no longer see the beauty that is out there, the beauty in Wilma

Bishop's caring, the beauty in Ann Plymouth's smile and in the way she wants me for her child, the beauty in all that Hans and Ivan and Bessie Delany have done and are doing and will ever do.

But the water boils and the bubbles burst across the surface, and I open my eyes and I look into the street below and I can see more clearly.

My father asks if I regret the life I have lived, and I answer him. He asks what I intend to do with this life I am so happy with, and for this one I have no reply because I am caught, the same as we all are caught, between our two lives, our two histories: the ones we've lived, and the ones we might have lived; and caught as well between the world of theory and the world of practice, our public selves and the selves we live with in private.

When I open my eyes, the man is still beating the woman. When I open my eyes, I cannot close them again until I decide who I am.

There are ways of coming back. There are ways to make a presence known and felt. Perhaps to someone a visible presence might count for something.

It is awfully naive of me to think that my coming back to Harlem means anything to anyone but me and perhaps to the few people whose lives have touched mine, naive to think that my white-silk-trousered presence makes any difference at all, that Harlem would not be what it has become if I had stayed. Perhaps it is the opposite that is true, that I would not be who I am if I had remained here. My sensibilities would be different, and all that I have seen along these streets and from this window would seem normal to me. There is beauty in Harlem, much beauty in being black, but my vision has been clouded by the outside world I have seen and become a part of. I have trouble seeing the beauty sometimes.

No, it is not outside my window this night. There is nothing lovely in one man stabbing another, no joy in a man beating a woman, but beauty does exist on these streets somewhere, and the only way to find it, perhaps, is simply to look for it, perhaps even more simply to create it.

I could turn my back, of course, could indeed refuse to be black, could even refuse to care and just go back to bed, flee once more to the suburbs or go back to the south of France, but that would be too easy. And perhaps in time that is what I will do: take my rightful place in the world of all men and women and settle for nothing but that which speaks to my own individual soul, and win the battle fought by my father and by Eliot Winston's grandfather and by the countless nameless black men and women. Perhaps in time I can indeed refuse to be black, refuse to give blackness more relevance than it deserves, refuse to see myself in such narrow terms, and refuse to let others decide for me who I am and the course of my actions. Perhaps in time the things done by other black men will cast no shadow onto me and no reflection and I will not see myself in what they do.

One day, perhaps, but not this night. This night I am here. This night I am black and I am in Harlem and I have no choice but to be in this moment and make of it what I can. I have to be who I am, who I was that night, split in two once more and torn between what I want to do and what I ought to do, and that night I could wait no longer for the police or anyone else to come.

Quickly, then, I slid into my jeans and slipped a T-shirt over my head. I put on my socks and shoes and I went downstairs.

I ran into Herbert Washington a few days later. He was smiling that old-man smile of his, which turned into a big grin when I told him about the other evening and how my heart had quietly thumped as I went down to the street. I had surprised myself. I had been a little nervous but unafraid. Still, I had taken my time getting dressed, hoping that by the time I reached the street the quarreling couple would have left. When I arrived, they were still there. I crossed the street slowly and approached them.

"You should have been shaking like crazy. I would have been," Herbert said. "Too many people these days got guns. Too many people don't mind using them."

That same thought had crossed my mind more than twice as I left the apartment, went down the stairs and out into the street. Certainly I wanted to be a hero; it is how I see myself. I was in no mood, however, for heroics.

"What do you want then?" the man said. He barked when he spoke. His voice, high-pitched and weak, snapped sharply.

"You want a piece of this," he said, meaning the woman, "or you want a piece of me?"

What I wanted I could not express. What I wanted, I was not sure myself. I wanted to be back in bed, that much I did know. I wanted the clock turned back, wanted not to have been disturbed from my sleep. I would have known nothing, would have had to make no decisions, take no action. Once awakened, I had to decide who I was, who I wanted to be, who I was going to be.

"I don't want a piece of anything," I said. "I just want to be left alone."

"What you doing here then? What you want? What you looking at?"

"I'm just looking at you," I said.

Everything I did, I did deliberately. I was trying to figure out what to do. I spoke slowly and softly. I separated each sentence by a pause that seemed minutes long.

"I'm just watching you, just watching what you do. I want to know what you look like. I want to remember your face."

"Get on away from here," he shouted. "Ain't nobody messing with you."

"Yeah, well," I said. "You know how it is."

He was softening, showing a touch of fear. He could see that I was not going away. Although I couldn't see if he had a gun, he would have at least shown it by now if he did have one. Nonetheless, I stood behind a car. He had backed away from the woman, and all of his attention was on me now. I stayed in the street and used the car as my shield. He took a step in my direction.

"What are you: brave?"

"Not me," I said. "I'm not going to do anything to you. I'm not even going to try. I just want to be here while you do what you do. I want to witness it. That's all I can do. I want to see if you're as pathetic as you look, so pathetic you don't care about anything. I want to know if you can keep it up with somebody looking on. I want you to see the disgust in my face. I want to remind myself and I want to remind you that there's nothing about you that I want to be like, and nobody else wants to be like you either. I already know it, but I want you to know it too."

Herbert Washington grinned broadly, his milky eyes wide open, his head tossed back a little. He had about him that know-everything aspect of an old man, as if he knew everything before I said anything—and more than that, as if he had somehow been the cause of it all.

"You said all that?" In his voice was a mixture of amazement and admiration. "You must be crazy."

"Yeah, I must be," I said. "But what would you expect me to do: pretend I didn't see what was going on, toss my hands up, and give up on them both just like that?"

"That's what I would have done," he said. "That's what most people would have done."

"Yeah, well." I couldn't think of anything else to say.

"Then what happened? What did he say next?"

"The usual," I said. "He threatened to kill me. He said if he ever saw me again he was going to pop me."

He had wanted to pop me right then, he had said.

"If I'd be strapped I would have popped you by now," he shouted. He was moving on down the road now, the woman moving right along with him. He was screaming and cussing all the while, now at me, now and again at the woman. I followed along until they had stumbled down to 130th Street and over to Amsterdam Avenue. Beneath the bright lights on that corner, they calmed down. He was still scowling at me, but he put his arm around the woman's waist and held her up. She was holding on with both arms. He reached out his left hand and pointed down into the street. A gypsy cab stopped; the man and the woman fell inside and shut the door.

"I'm going to remember you," he said. "I better not ever see your ass around here. If I see you again, I'm going to kill you."

"And then what? And then what?" Herbert said. He was like a child caught in the twists of a good bedtime story.

"Well," I said. "I guess I'm still here."

He smiled and settled back against the wall of his building.

"Yeah," he said. "I guess you are."

He looked up and down the avenue. Then he looked at me with such expectation that I knew it was my turn to speak.

"Are you going to tell me now?" I asked.

"Tell you what?" Now he was nonchalant.

"You know. You said you would tell me what I needed to know about Harlem, what's wrong, what's right. You said you would tell me all the answers."

"I did?"

"You did," I said. "You said you would tell me what I needed to know."

"Ach!" he said with a broad slow wave of his arm. "You don't need me to tell you anything; you already know it."

I scanned head and heart to see what he meant, what I might possibly have known or could have learned. All I could think of at that moment was a man I met one time on a train to Chicago. He too had lived in Harlem and had gotten out—escaped, he said, through hard work and perseverance. He got into the real estate business, made a lot of money, bought low, sold high, and moved out of Harlem.

"All the time I lived there," he said, "I never once believed I would be trapped there. I never believed that Harlem was all there was to life, and I wanted a piece of what was out there in the great wide world. Just because I'm black does not mean I'm supposed to be satisfied. It's a white man's country, a white man's world only if we allow it to be."

There was another man who once said that although he lived in the ghetto, the ghetto did not live in him. It is a line I have heard many times before and is, I imagine, a way of saying that you can overcome physical circumstance with a state of mind. I suppose that's true, but I wonder sometimes how you can separate where you've been from where you are from where you're headed. I'm not sure you should even want to.

Once again I ask myself if I ever really left Harlem and now have been trying to get back. Or was I simply never able to leave in the first place?

There is, I know for sure now, no way out. Once you have

experienced anything so deeply, there can be no going back, no forgetting, no way to live without its being inside you. You can leave it, but you can never get away. You may rise above the ghetto. You may tell yourself—and probably should—that you live in it but are not of it, but although attitude is important, I know it is not the only thing. You cannot ignore the bars and walls of your personal prisons. Otherwise there would be nothing to rise above, nothing to overcome.

Nor can you live within the walls of any culture and not be a product of that culture, unless you live encased completely in a cocoon. How can you deny the influence of the world around you, deny that it affects you or that it in some way shapes you? How can you separate who you have become from the forces that made you, even as the world around you attempts to reduce you to the stereotype of your smaller world and treat you accordingly?

In a sense, then, we carry Harlem the way we carry our blackness. There is no escaping either one. The ghetto lies within.

Ralph Ellison once said that Harlem has a way of expanding, that it goes where black folks go. He was not talking only about the physical boundaries of place. He lived technically in Washington Heights, the next neighborhood up from here, but as many did then and still do, he called it Harlem because there were so many black people there. Wherever sufficient numbers of blacks gather to live, there Harlem is. Perhaps it is Harlem with only two, perhaps with only one.

I have lived in Harlem, I guess, since I was a little boy.

―――――

On the street one day I spoke to the man from the apartment across the way. He had stopped me to bum a cigarette and we started talking about the noisiness of the neighborhood. I told him about a couple across the little courtyard from me, told him about the drunken arguments, and laughed at how each fight ends with the man getting thrown out.

"Always, always," I said. "Then he's back for more the next time."

I recognized him then even before he said anything. He lowered his eyes and was embarrassed.

"That would be me," he said.

We chatted a few minutes more about the weather and about baseball, and finally I could pretend to ignore his secret no more and I asked him.

"You guys get drunk every weekend night. You spend hours and hours hollering at each other. It's a wonder you haven't killed her yet."

"Or that she hasn't killed me," he said.

"Every time she throws you out."

He nodded.

"Every time you come back."

He nodded, just as gravely, but there was a tiny smile creeping into his lips.

"Why?" I asked. "Why do you keep coming back?"

He almost laughed, but the smile disappeared and he was very serious.

"Because I love her," he said. "We're in this thing, and we're going to stay in this thing until we figure it out. I guess you could say we're trapped, prisoners of love, I suppose."

Now he laughed. He tossed his head back and he laughed and he laughed and he laughed. I laughed along with him until he turned away and walked down the street to try to bum from someone else the cigarette I did not have.

I watched him go. Then I turned and walked in the opposite direction, feeling unbearably light-headed and strangely at peace.

Me tenant comme je suis, Keeping myself as I am,
un pied dans un pays one foot in one country
et l'autre dans un autre, and the other in another,
je trouve ma condition I find my condition
très heureuse, a very happy one,
en ce qu'elle est libre. in that it is free.

—RENÉ DESCARTES